JAIPUR

10 EASY WALKS

Dharmendar Kanwar

Photographs by

N P Singh

Rupa & Co

For

Ma and Kanwarsa

Narayan Pratap and Abhijit

Text © Dharmendar Kanwar 2004

First Published 2004
Second Impression 2010

Published by

Rupa • Co

7/16, Ansari Road, Daryaganj
New Delhi 110 002

Sales Centres:

Allahabad Bengalooru Chandigarh Chennai
Hyderabad Jaipur Kathmandu
Kolkata Mumbai

Maps and line drawings by K P Singh.
Photographs:
The old black & white city pictures are courtesy Evelyn
Bazelgette. Other contributors are Sudhir Kasliwal,
A S Jhala, Narendra Sain and M D Sharma.

Designed & typeset by
Arrt Creations
45 Nehru Apts, Kalkaji
New Delhi 110 019

Printed in India by
Gopsons Papers Ltd., Noida

CONTENTS

ACKNOWLEDGEMENTS

I would like to thank Jaya Wheaton, well-known artist and a very dear friend for helping me in innumerable ways. She accompanied me on some of the walks and gave me very valid suggestions about the areas that *just had to be explored* by the visitor. Dr Chandramani Singh, an eminent art historian provided some valuable insights and also helped me get my historical facts right.

I had prepared a brochure on *one* Heritage Walk for Rajasthan Tourism several years ago that had been initiated by Debasish Naik, an Ahmedabad based conservation architect and an expert on Heritage Walks. It was under his guidance that the Department of Tourism identified their first walk and realised its potential.

I would also like to thank my husband — my in-house historian and guide on all matters pertaining to the rich and diverse culture of Rajasthan, and my staunchest critic — my son, for their patience as they sometimes walked with me and sometimes drove me around the city and waited for me to 'rediscover' the by-lanes of Jaipur.

A big thank you to all of you.

INTRODUCTION

This book is a tribute to the beautiful city of Jaipur and proposes to introduce the visitor to the city's fascinating inner areas. It is a city that never ceases to amaze. Consider this — today we have our planning departments equipped to take on the most complicated designing projects. We plan housing colonies and industrial areas, the best of technical know-how is available and our designers have access to the latest computers. And what have we created? Is there anything even half as impressive as the city of Jaipur? What did Sawai Jai Singh have in the early eighteenth century except a vision? Yet, he designed a city so perfect, so beautiful, the likes of which cannot be found the world over. Not a single aspect of designing has been overlooked here, from the uniformity of the shops to the length and breadth of the streets. Houses were placed strategically so that the hot summer sun was blocked out, yet they received adequate sunlight and air. Proper sewage lines were laid and the wells ensured that no house went without its share of water. One does wonder how Sawai Jai Singh could visualise, in the eighteenth century, the needs of the city. It was the genius of the ruler that not only did he design a perfect city but he also made provisions for its future expansion. What kind of instructions must he have given to his planner Vidyadhar Bhattacharya? How did he explain the different *mohallas*, the *chaupars* where the general public could relax, the temples that were placed just outside the lanes and the sections that were demarcated for different communities? And how did Vidyadhar Bhattacharya manage to follow the guidelines and execute them so perfectly? Not a lane, not a house, not a wall is out of proportion. Did those visionaries know that they were giving shape to a city that would become a marvel in town planning and that the most experienced of architects would visit the city to try and learn something from it?

The streets with their treasures of scalloped arches, dainty pillared cupolas make Jaipur, with its enclosing wall and seven gates, a tourist's delight.

These walks have been planned in a way that they allow you to get a glimpse into the enchanting city and its charmingly chaotic life but they are by no means comprehensive. Every lane in the walled city has something interesting to offer and these walks take you into most of the city's important blocks or **chowkris** from **Chowkri Topkhana Desh** to **Chokri Ramchandraji.** Sadly though, most of the temples mentioned are being partly reused as schools, colleges and shops.

Availability of public transport has been kept in mind and care has also been taken to keep to the main streets. Though it is perfectly safe to go into the by-lanes, it is advisable not to venture alone.

Do keep in mind the fact that there are still a lot of areas that these walks do not cover and a there's a lot left to explore, to learn and to do.

Nataniyon ki Haveli

HISTORY

Jaipur is a city of many colours and contrasts. It is best explored at a leisurely pace, as there is so much to see and do that a usual taxi or bus tour can never do justice to Sawai Jai Singh II's planned city built in AD 1727.

Jai Singh visualised it as a flourishing centre of commerce and art with a special area designated for the different trades and crafts. Vidyadhar Bhattacharya, based the layout keeping in mind the principles of the Hindu treatise on architecture, the *Vastu Shastra*. The meticulous planning, the right combination of commerce and beauty, attracted visitors from all over the world.

Come and see for yourself what led Louis Rousselet, a well-known nineteenth century French traveller to comment, "The town is built in a style of unusual magnificence.... I doubt whether at the time it was built there were many cities in Europe which could compare with it."

The walks will introduce you to many of Jaipur's best-known monuments that are still located inside the old walled city. Enter any of the lanes leading from the main streets and each one will unfold several interesting facets of Jaipur's traditional lifestyle, architecture, arts, crafts, community living, havelies and temples.

As you explore all this and more, you realise that it is not just a city of forts, palaces and gardens.

It is a culturally rich city that has happily accepted t-shirts, jeans and baseball caps along with traditional turbans, *dhotis* and *ghagras* (traditional skirts) - they're all a part of this live, throbbing, exuberant city.

A city like this is still hard to come by.

ABOUT THE WALKS

The walled city will throw many more surprises if explored on foot or cycle rickshaw. Except for increased crowds and many more motorised vehicles than before, nothing seems to have changed here. Today, the streets of the city are crowded with buses, cars, bicycles, motorcycles as well as camel and bullock carts fighting for their space on the roads. It may interest you to know that at any given time you can see thirteen different modes of transportation - the highest in the country. But it is still an enchanting maze of streets, exhilarating, at times infuriating, crowded, colourful but never dull.

For the first-time visitor, Jaipur is definitely a feast for the eyes because life in the walled city still has the flavour and ambience of old times. Despite having grown into a bustling metropolis, the ancient heart of this planned city still beats in its *gali-mohallas* rather than the beautiful palaces. Along the route of the walks, you will find many warm and friendly people who will

happily welcome you into their homes and give you a cup of tea and tell you stories of the days gone by. In fact, you will also come across several areas where elderly people sit together outside teashops and discuss anything from politics to the good old times. Look out — and avoid, youngsters sometimes posing as students who may promise to get you good bargains.

Be prepared for the unexpected, in sights, sounds and smells. Chaotic and noisy, people jostling against each other, stray cows butting in, lots of bargaining...

opp: A picture of Nataniyon ki Haveli from the year 1908.
A view of Johari Bazaar in the early twentieth century.

THE INTRICACIES OF TOWN PLANNING

The more you discover the city, the more you come to appreciate and marvel at Vidyadhar Bhattacharya's town planning talents. He divided the area available to him in rectangular blocks or *chowkris*. The palace complex occupied two of these nine blocks, which was approximately one seventh of the total city area. The other seven blocks were given equal, if not more, attention and had beautiful buildings lining the wide streets. Each area had a clearly defined line of construction, the permissible height as well as elevation of the building.

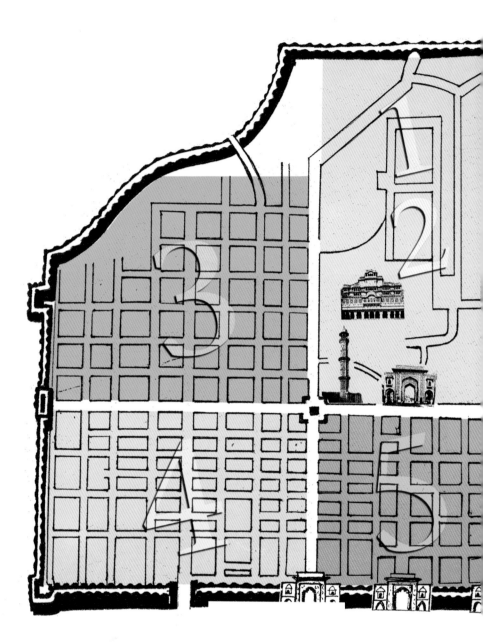

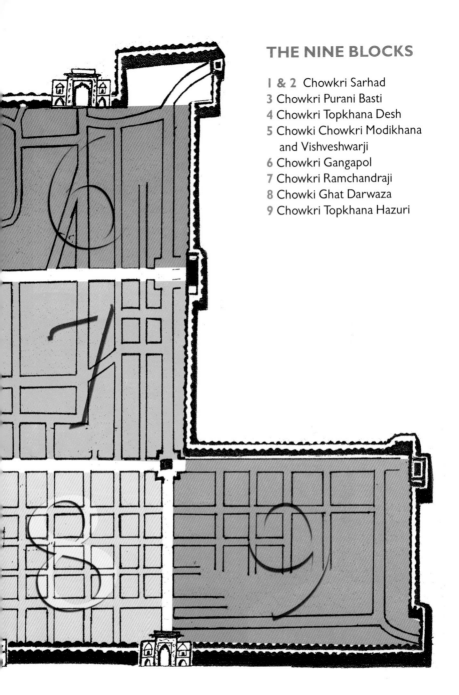

THE NINE BLOCKS

1 & 2 Chowkri Sarhad
3 Chowkri Purani Basti
4 Chowkri Topkhana Desh
5 Chowki Chowkri Modikhana
and Vishveshwarji
6 Chowkri Gangapol
7 Chowkri Ramchandraji
8 Chowki Ghat Darwaza
9 Chowkri Topkhana Hazuri

a block combining Chowkri **Modikhana** and **Vishveshwarji** was designated for use by rich Jain and Hindu businessmen and other officials. Most of the city's old families still maintain their ancestral havelies here.

Chowkri Sarhad was the palace block with temples, gardens and other royal buildings. Other *chowkris* were **Purani Basti** that was earmarked for residences of leading courtiers; **Topkhana Desh** was for the *Thikanedars* around Jaipur, chiefs of the state's divisions;

Merchants occupied one part of **Ghat Darwaza** while artists and workers occupied the other parts. **Chokri Ramchandraji** contained important temples and havelies built by maharajas, maharanis and leading nobles. Located on the north east of this *chowkri* were small residences of royal staff and craftsmen. These *chowkries* were further divided into smaller wards and sub-wards.

Top: Sireh Deorhi Gate.
View of the city from Nahargarh.

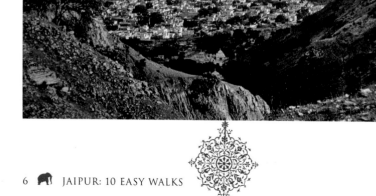

The least developed were **Topkhana Hazuri** and **Chowkri Gangapol** because these were later additions. While the former was uneven and sandy, used for the artillery of the ruler and by poor artisans, the latter was used mainly by labourers. When you walk through these *chowkries* you will notice that these are still not as well developed or designed as the rest of the city.

The new city was enclosed by a fortified wall 20 feet in height and 9 feet in width and pierced by seven (considered an auspicious Indian number) major gates, similar in design with a large central opening flanked by two smaller ones on either side. The gates are **Suraj Pol, Chand Pol, Ram Pol, Shiv Pol,** **Kishan Pol, Ganga Pol** and **Dhruv Pol. Man Pol,** better known as New Gate, was a later addition.

You will go through most of them, so do look out for the huge wooden gates with metal strips (for added strength) and guardrooms built into the central opening. These were not just decorative gates but had a very important function. They were closed at night for protection against intruders and wild animals that roamed outside the walls. This happened till early twentieth century and there are people still living who remember those days.

Interestingly, the walled city has needed very few changes from the time it was planned by Sawai Jai Singh. Even today there is

ample room for pedestrian as well as mounted traffic. In the eighteenth century, Jai Singh had decided that the main streets in the city would be approximately 110 feet wide. That is the width of the straight road between the **Suraj Pol** (Sun Gate in the east) and **Chand Pol** (Moon Gate in the west). Three major streets of equal width cut across neatly at right angles and divide the area into neat blocks. The three *choupars* (squares), or intersections thus formed are — **Badi Chaupad, Choti Chaupad** and **Ramganj Chaupad** that make highly interesting community and traffic centres. The area is further divided by secondary streets half that width and minor ones that are one fourth of the main artery.

Another noteworthy feature that makes Jaipur unique is the fact that because the rulers were great patrons of art and craft, they encouraged craftsmen to come and settle in Jaipur. Specific areas were allocated to potters, stone carvers, dyers, jewellers, painters, kite makers, weavers and so on - a tradition that has survived to this day. Jaipur is still known the world over as a major craft destination and has a mind-boggling range of crafts to offer. It is a favourite not only with the casual shopper but the international design fraternity as well. A lot of major fashion houses head towards Jaipur when they need good quality work done in garments or in furniture, jewellery etc.

From the first ruler of Jaipur (not Amber) Sawai Jai Singh II in 1699 to the tenth Maharaja Man Singh II who died in 1970, each ruler contributed to the city's development, both culturally as well as architecturally. By the time the present Maharaja Brigadier Bhawani Singh came to power in 1970, the curtain had fallen on the golden era of Maharajas and their palaces and power shifted to the democratic government that took over the reigns of the country.

THE MAHARAJAS OF JAIPUR

A brief look at the city's 276 year-old history will give you a fair idea of the city's development. Each period of history made it's own contribution to this thriving city.

Sawai Jai Singh II died in 1743, sixteen years after he had founded the city, and was succeeded by his son **Ishwari Singh** (r. 1743-1750)

Ishwari Singh

who in his brief reign of seven years patronised many literary works; had a beautiful *chhatri* erected in his father's memory, built the **Moti Burj** in Chaugan and the impressive seven-storied **Ishwar Lat** or **Swarga Suli** in Tripolia.

Sawai Jai Singh II

Madho Singh I

Prithvi Singh (r. 1767-78) came to the throne at the tender age of five and died at the age of sixteen when he fell off a horse. He never did get to do much as his stepmother Chandrawatji and her trusted ministers held the power. The eleven years of his reign were full of conspiracies and political strife.

Madho Singh I (r. 1750-1767) was the brother of Ishwari Singh and came to the throne after a bitter and decisive battle with the latter. He was a large man at 6 ½ feet and weighed over 250 kg. In the seventeen years of his rule, he tried to wipe out the infamy connected to his accession. He made a remarkable contribution in several fields from art and architecture to religion and literature. He founded the city of **Sawai Madhopur**; built the **Madho Niwas** and **Diwan-I-Am** in the City Palace; **Madho Vilas** near Zorawar Singh Gate (where Maharani Gayatri Devi started her MGD Girls Public School, now an Ayurveda College); the **Jal Mahal Palace** on Amber Road and the **Sisodia Rani Ka Bagh** on Agra Road.

Prithvi Singh

Pratap Singh (r. 1778-1803) was Chandrawatji's own son and took over as Maharaja at the age of fourteen. He wrote poetry under the name of *Brijnidhi* and was a great devotee of Lord Krishna. He constructed eight temples devoted to Him – the important ones being **Brijnidhiji, Anandkrishna Behari, Anand Behariji** and **Madan Mohanji**. He constructed the

Pratap Singh

fountains behind the Govinddevji temple. But he is remembered more for building the most famous monument of Jaipur – the **Hawa Mahal**.

Jagat Singh (r. 1803-1818) ruled for fifteen years but his reign is marked more for his love life than reforms of any kind. His twenty-one wives and twenty-four concubines gave him little time to devote to the affairs of the state. He became obsessed with a courtesan by the name of Ras Kapoor and wanted to make her the maharani of half his kingdom causing a lot of discontent amongst his courtiers.

Jai Singh III (r. 1818-1835) was a minor who ruled under the minority council that was guided by the East India Company. He died under mysterious circumstances without making any significant contribution.

Jai Singh III

He was followed by one of the most remarkable rulers of Jaipur - **Ram Singh II** (r. 1835-1880) who was also a minor when he came to the throne. This enlightened ruler was a great patron of art and learning, a photographer and an

Jagat Singh

able administrator whose rule is known as the golden age of Jaipur. Listing his various administrative reforms and contribution to the state would require a separate book in itself. In fact, the Maharaja was known to wander around in the streets at night to apprise himself of the condition of the poor and the destitute. In the forty-five years of his rule, he made innumerable public buildings and set up offices

Madho Singh II

Ram Singh II

to give better education, roads, lights and water supply. He is remembered today for major works of public utility, most of which have survived over the years.

Some of his important buildings are the **Town Hall, Mayo Hospital, Ram Niwas Garden** and **Albert Hall Museum, Ram**

Prakash Theatre and **Maharaja School of Arts & Crafts.**

Ram Singh II adopted **Madho Singh II** (r. 1880-1922) from a nearby village called Isarda. He was an orthodox Hindu and undertook steps to improve the irrigation, railways and education system of Jaipur. However, he is best remembered for the wrong reasons – the size of his harem — he had five wives, eighteen official mistresses and at the time of his death there were five thousand concubines and eunuchs in the *zenana*. The well known courtesans of that time were Durga, Shirin, Lalan, Khairan and Gohar Jan. He was invited to England in 1901 for the coronation of King Edward VII and he travelled by a liner called S.S. *Olympia* that was redesigned to include a Krishna temple. He also took two huge silver urns containing holy water from the Ganges River. The holy water transported all the way to England in the 349 kg silver urns was enough to last him until his visit overseas.

Man Singh II (r. 1922-1949) was the second son of Thakur Sawai Singh of Isarda and was adopted by Madho Singh II at the age of ten. He was a world-class

Man Singh II

polo player and widely recognised as the father of new Jaipur. He went on to become the Rajpramukh of Rajasthan and later the ambassador to Spain. Among his many notable contributions to Jaipur were the construction of the **Zenana Hospital**, the **Maharaja's**

and **Maharani's Colleges, SMS Hospital, Medical College, Rajasthan University, Moti Doongri, Lily Pool**, modifications to the **Rambagh Palace** and the present **Secretariat**. He married **Maharani Gayatri Devi** who was famed for her beauty and is mentioned in the Guinness Book of World Records for winning an election by the highest majority ever. He died in 1970 while playing polo in Cirencester, England.

Maharani Gayatri Devi

Maharaja (Brigadier) Bhawani Singh continues to reside in the City Palace with his family and has had to come to terms with the changing times. He is a much-decorated soldier of the Indian Army and was awarded a Mahavir Chakra, the second highest

Maharaja (Brigadier) Bhawani Singh

gallantry award, for his role in the 1971 Indo-Pak war. He takes a keen interest in the running of the City Palace Museum.

ROMANCE OF PINK

When the city was planned and built, it was a plain cream colour and remained so for over a century. There are various stories as to the origin of the pink colour but one that is largely agreed upon by historians is the one to do with the visit of the Prince of Wales in 1876. Maharaja Ram Singh II wanted the city to look clean and new to welcome his guest and experimented with different shades for different streets. Several colours

Maharaja Man Singh II with a guest.

a little confused with the various pinks ranging from an ice cream pink to bright terracotta red, but it is a city that is still trying to get its original shade right!

were tried and rejected and the terracotta pink was the final choice for the main shopping area. The colour stayed and gave Jaipur its name – Pink City.

A typical street scene in the walled city.

Today there are municipal regulations that have made it mandatory for the house owners within the walled city to paint their buildings in the approved shade of pink. The visitor, however, may get

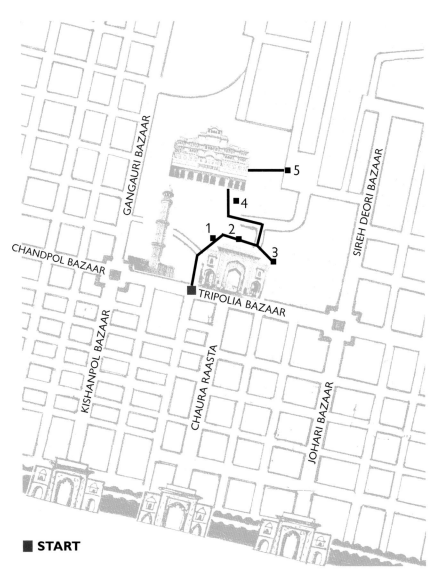

■ START

WALK I

1. Brijnidhi Temple
2. Shri Anand Krishna Behariji Temple
3. Jantar Mantar
4. City Palace
5. Jaleb Chowk

WALK 1

CHANDINI CHOWK — JANTAR MANTAR — CITY PALACE

This is the heart of the walled city — the **Sarhad Chowkri** occupies two of the nine squares and covers one-seventh area of the entire walled city. Go into the huge courtyard just outside the City Palace. Then to the Jantar Mantar where you can learn about the movement of planets and study time on a huge sundial, amongst other interesting things; then move on to the beautiful palace complex where you could easily spend almost half the day browsing around Sawai Man Singh II Museum.

PARKING

Leave your car or scooter/cycle rickshaw at the Chandini Chowk just behind the Tripolia Gate. There is enough parking here. Your car can wait here or meet you outside the side gate of City Palace that opens into the Jaleb Chowk.

PLACES OF INTEREST

Chandini Chowk – Brijnidhi Temple – Pratapeshwar Mandir – Shri Anand Krishna Behariji Mandir – Jantar Mantar – City Palace

THE WALK

The sheer size of **Chandini Chowk** will surprise you as you come in through the crowded market. There is a huge open space, no traffic to dodge and most importantly, it is peaceful. As you stand with the Tripolia Gate behind you, you will find three temples here. The temples on the left are those of **Pratapeshwarji** and **Brijnidhiji**. Just behind the latter is the famous **Janani Deori**, the

Chandni Chowk

chamber of the royal ladies. Each maharani had her own apartment here. **Rajmata Gayatri Devi** still continues to keep her section, *rawala*, which she visits quite often. It is a world in itself but unfortunately one is not allowed access to it. Instead, explore the temples.

MANDIR SHRI BRIJNIDHIJI

Maharaja Pratap Singh constructed this temple in 1792 after he dreamt that **Govind Devji** wanted him to make a new temple of **Shri Brijnidhiji** in his palace.

The temple has been built in a haveli style with a huge courtyard. Tread carefully as years of disuse have made the structure quite dilapidated.

As you leave this temple the one on your right, next to the gate is **Mandir Shri Pratapeshwar.** On your left is the inner gate leading to City Palace and on your right is

Idol of Brijnidhi

Walk out and turn right and keep going until you get to a small gate that will lead you to a garden that looks straight out of a science fiction movie with the most unusual collection of stone and lime mortar structures. This is the famous **Jantar Mantar**. The ticket window is near the entrance. It is a good idea to take one of the several

the rear side of Tripolia Gate. You will see guards posted here as these gates are not meant for the general public. Only the maharaja of Jaipur and his family can use them. It is an accepted fact and a tradition respected by the local people. Interestingly, several years ago a politician's son decided to break this tradition and insisted on driving right through this gate only to meet with a fatal accident soon after. No politician has since attempted to use the gate without royal approval and sanction!

guides available there because it won't be much fun unless you learn the different functions of each of these unusual structures.

Walk straight ahead and you will see another huge temple in this courtyard. This is the **Anand Krishna Behariji temple** and worth a visit.

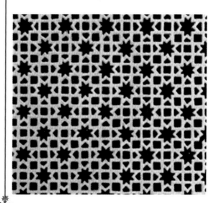

Top: Detail from Brijnidhi temple
Right: Anand Krishna Behariji temple

JANTAR MANTAR

Sawai Jai Singh II built the Jantar Mantar, or Observatory in 1728. He was an enthusiastic astronomer and spent much time and money on building this observatory, which is still one of Jaipur's main attractions. Jai Singh had it built complex. The function of each instrument is rather complex but serves a particular function where time plays the main theme.

Jai Singh was aware that astronomical instruments being used in other parts of the world were smaller in size but his careful study led him to believe that the small, metal instruments were not

An aerial view of Jantar Mantar

just outside the City Palace – close enough for him to spend hours indulging in the study of the skies. He used it daily, often with his astronomy gurus Pandit Jagannath and Kewal Ram. In all, there are seventeen instruments in this accurate enough. After studying all available works on astronomy, he successfully designed these gigantic stone and masonry instruments and made efforts to improve upon them. Emissaries were sent to meet other astronomers and obtain the latest and the most advanced astronomical instruments. This is amazing when you realise that all this was happening in the eighteenth century. Those were times when wars were being fought; maharajas were more interested in expanding their kingdoms or living in regal splendour than in studying the planets. But Jai Singh II was an extraordinary man.

These fascinating architectural innovations were designed and built to measure astronomical quantities such as such as declinations, altitudes, eclipses, time, etc. of the sun, moon, and other planets at different times of the year. Amazingly, this astounding collection of complex instruments is still in use today even after almost three hundred years. Every year, astrologers gather here just before the rains, make their readings and predict the kind of monsoon Jaipur can expect. It does seem to work!

He built five of these in other parts of the country – Delhi, Ujjain, Mathura, and Varanasi. This observatory is the largest and the best preserved – and a fitting tribute to the great astronomer king.

Do not be in a hurry to rush through the Jantar Mantar complex. Take your time and let the guide give you a detailed tour. The complex also has a newly built

Jantar Mantar

Narivalaya Yantra

museum where miniature models of all the large instruments are displayed. The City Palace Museum is also a good place to see old plans and manuscripts pertaining to the Observatory.

Brief descriptions about the different instruments are given for your information.

SAMRAT YANTRA

This Supreme Instrument is the largest and the most important. It is a sun-dial 90 feet high and 148 feet wide. Its shadow on one of the two quadrants, which lie in a plane parallel to the equator, gives the local solar time.

NARIVALAYA YANTRA

This 3.05 metre cylindrical dial indicates time and hemisphere. There is an iron peg in the centre of the flat stone disc. As the shadow moves around the peg it is possible to take readings and ascertain the time of the day.

YANTRA RAJ

This is an astrolabe, made of many alloys to withstand any change in the temperatures. This huge metal disc rests on a wooden beam. There is a hole at the centre through which one can ascertain the position of the Pole star.

Jaiprakasha Yantra

KRANTI VRITTA YANTRA

This slightly complicated instrument is a combination of stone and brass. It helps to determine the latitude and longitude of stars and planets.

UNNATANSHA YANTRA

This large brass circle has diameters intersecting each other at right angles and was used for finding altitudes.

RASHIVALAYA YANTRA

These are twelve instruments, each of which represents a sign of the Zodiac. All these twelve instruments are based on the larger Samrat Yantra and helped to make accurate horoscopes.

JAIPRAKASHA YANTRA

This is made up of two complimentary parts. There is a round metal disc with a hole at the center. The position of the sun is determined by the shadow of the intersection falling on the hemisphere.

KAPALI YANTRA

This purpose of this instrument was to reckon the altitude of azimuth meridian and pass time.

Ram Yantra

RAM YANTRA

This Yantra looks like a pillared room without a roof. In the middle, there is another pillar that divides the floor into sectors to allow easy observation. These are meant to measure the altitude and azimuth of the sun.

Walk out of the Observatory and go straight ahead. The building across the road on your left is the City Palace. The entrance, **Gainda ki Deorhi,** is on your left and the ticket window to the right of this gate.

The plan of the City Palace is similar to the plan of the city. In a way, it is a city within a city. It has a high wall or the **sarhad** that surrounds it on all sides and several gates leading to the main palace. **Gainda ki Deorhi** will take you

The Diwan-i-Khas

into a large courtyard in the middle of which sits the white marble and pink sand stone **Mubarak Mahal** (Palace of Welcome).

Quite a bit of information is printed on the ticket itself but if you want a more interesting and animated commentary then you should take a guide.  These approved City Palace guides can give you authentic information.

MUBARAK MAHAL

Sir Samuel Swinton Jacob designed this two-storied building in 1890 as a rest house for Maharaja Madho Singh II (1880-1922). It was later used as the **Mahakma Khas** (Royal Secretariat) and is now the **Tosha Khana** (royal wardrobe) of the museum. The museum offices are located on the ground floor.

The first floor houses fine muslins, silks, local hand printed cottons and embroidered coats from north India. Do not miss the *atamsukh* (long quilted robe) of Madho Singh I (r. 1750-67). Made from gold-encrusted pink silk, it covered his huge frame (6 ½ feet and 250 kilos). Also on display here is the gold embroidered *lehanga-choli* worn by one of the Jaipur maharanis at her wedding.

Walk out of the Mubarak Mahal and head towards the east

Mubarak Mahal

Display of swords from the armoury.

side to the Arms and Armoury Museum (**Sileh Khana**) in the **Anand Mahal**. It houses a fine collection of Indian antique weaponry – pistols, blunderbusses, flintlocks, swords, rifles and daggers. The weapon collection also includes the massive sword of Maharaja Man Singh I that weighs at least eleven pounds, a turban shaped helmet belonging to Mirza Raja Jai Singh I and the unique dagger that has two miniature pistols built into its handle. This was once the common room of the harem, and has a beautiful view of the **Chandra Mahal** from its first floor windows.

Right outside the Mubarak Mahal stands the **Rajendra Pol** flanked by two elephants, each of them carved from a single block of marble. In 1931, they were brought here from the *zenana* (women's quarters) to mark the birth of Maharaja Bhawani Singh who was the first direct male heir to the Jaipur throne in two generations. It follows the typical Hindu gatehouse architecture lavishly decorated with carved marble. It has ornate brackets, carved balconies, and brass studded doors. This is one of the most photographed areas of City Palace and visitors cannot seem to resist photographing the impressive guards here with their spotless white uniforms, red turbans and big moustaches.

Gangajali, the huge silver urn.

The **Rajendra Pol** takes you to a huge courtyard and into the central building, the **Sarvatobhadra** or the **Diwan-i-Khas** (c. 1730). This courtyard reflects the influence of Mughal architecture with a few Hindu features added to give an Indian touch. The **Diwan-i-Khas** is a large marble pillared hall set in a deep pink courtyard. There are several arches that support its decorated pavilion roof. This courtyard is very popular with Hindi film producers and numerous song sequences have been shot here.

You cannot miss the *pièce de résistance* here – the huge silver urns used by Sawai Madho Singh to carry water to England. These urns, better known as *Gangajali,*

measure five feet in height and are listed in the Guinness Book of Records as the largest single silver objects in the world.

When you have your back towards Rajendra Pol, on your left is the double storied **Ridhisidhi Pol** that leads to the **Pritam Niwas Chowk,** with its four beautiful gates. The **Peacock Gate** is the most famous of the gates depicting seasons and has painted stucco peacocks. Towards the north of **Pritam Niwas Chowk** lies the original palace building **Chandra Mahal** (Moon Palace), the **Zenana**

Peacock Gate

View of Chandra Mahal from Jaleb Chowk

Originally, **Chandra Mahal** was a single storied palace and the later kings added more floors. The building now has seven storeys and each floor is a luxurious, opulent palace by itself.

The main sections are the **Sukh Niwas**, or the House of Pleasure, the **Rang Mandir** and the **Sobha Niwas**. The **Shri Niwas** popularly called the **Sheesh Mahal** (Palace of Mirrors) is a huge room whose walls and ceilings are coated with coloured glass inlay, floral designs in gilt and also has elaborate stucco patterns on its pillars and ceiling. **Chhavi Niwas** presents a calm and serene picture in turquoise, indigo and white. The topmost floor is a smaller open pavilion called **Mukut Mahal**, or the crown palace. It has a beautiful curvilinear Bengal styled roof.

(Queen's Palace) on its northwest and the **Anand Mahal** on its south. To the west of the Chandra Mahal just beyond a small courtyard is **Madho Niwas** built by Madho Singh I that was later extended by his successor.

CHANDRA MAHAL

The **Chandra Mahal** is the earliest building of the palace complex and dominates the **Pritam Niwas Chowk**. The present maharaja and his family still continue to live here and most of it is not open to visitors.

Sarvatobhadra or the Diwan-i-Khas

When you come out of Pritam Niwas Chowk and with your back towards the **Sarvatobhadra**, the high eastern wall of the courtyard has two smaller gates, which lead to the **Sabha Niwas** or the **Diwan-i-Am,** the **Art Gallery** and the **Transport Gallery.**

DIWAN-I-AM

Maharaja Sawai Pratap Singh (1778-1803) built the **Diwan-i-Am** (Diwan Khana) or the Hall of Public Audience, at the end of the eighteenth century. The ceiling was painted in the 1870s and is highly decorated with floral motifs in gilt, green and red. This hall was designed for durbars and banquets and has

jaali screens behind which ladies in *purdah* could watch ceremonies. It has a picture gallery with an exquisite collection of Persian and Indian miniatures, royal carpets and an extensive collection of manuscripts. The **Diwan-i-Am** also houses one of India's largest chandeliers.

The other gate on the far right leads to the newly constructed Transport Gallery with its palanquins, chariots and buggies on display. On your north is **Ganesh Pol** that leads you out to the Jaleb Chowk.

How long you wish to spend here is entirely up to you. The walk ends here.

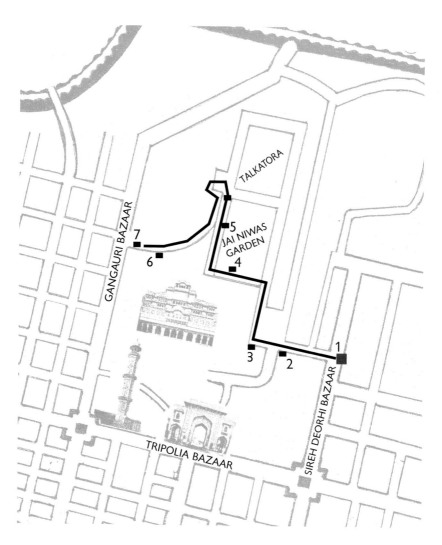

■ START

WALK 2

1. Sireh Deori Gate
2. Naqqarkhana Gate
3. Jaleb Chowk
4. Govinddevji Temple
5. Badal Mahal
6. Chini ki Burj
7. Chaugan

WALK 2

SIREH DEORI GATE — CHINI KI BURJ

A journey into the past – starting from the Sireh Deori Gate that leads to the City Palace complex. Go past the huge garages that house the **Indra Viman** – an elephant driven chariot, on to Jaleb Chowk that is part of the main square of the city that was used for ceremonial gatherings. See the Jaipur family's ruling deity and get a glimpse of a Mughal style garden.

PLACES OF INTEREST

Sireh Deori Gate – Naqqarkhana Gate – Jaleb Chowk – Govinddevji Temple – Jai Niwas Gardens – Badal Mahal – Talkatora – Chini ki Burj – Chaugan

PARKING

You can leave your car outside the **Sireh Deori Gate** (near Hawa Mahal) and have it wait for you just outside Chaugan Stadium. There is enough parking available on both ends of the walk so you have an option of starting from either point. Alternatively, public transport is easily available throughout the walk.

THE WALK

It is a good idea to begin this walk as early as you can because the sights and sounds of the morning are unusual and interesting.

Enter through this east-facing gate called **Sireh Deori Gate** that opens near the Hawa Mahal. Use of the south facing Tripolia Gate is restricted to the royal family but this is an equally important entry point and has been, ever since it was made. Go through this gate and it will get you to another, slightly smaller one called **Naqqarkhane ka Darwaza**.

NAQQARKHANE KA DARWAZA

In the days of the maharajas, the upper compartments of this fine gate were a venue for court musicians who announced arrivals and departures of maharajas and played the *"naubat"* eulogizing the chivalrous deeds of rulers past and present.

Today, the drums are silent and there is nothing to herald your entry into this most important of the city's blocks – except hundreds of pigeons that have got other things to do than spare you a look.

Between the two gates, there is an open space and as you walk in you will find yourself walking past these pigeons feeding almost in the middle of the road. Devout Hindus feed birds on a regular basis. A lot of people with a religious bent of mind come here to feed these pigeons; you too can do so if you wish. There are several temporary shops there with piles of grain that you can buy and scatter on the ground.

Naqqarkhane ka Darwaza

Indra Viman, Chariot of Lord Indra, a huge elephant carriage.

As you feed the pigeons, look towards your right and note the huge garages. They look almost like narrow, vertical hangars. They were meant to house the **Indra Viman**, Chariot of Lord Indra, a huge elephant carriage.

Walk in through this gate and it will get you into a large square called the **Jaleb Chowk** (or Parade Square) of the City Palace.

JALEB CHOWK

Jaleb is a distortion of a Persian word *Zaleb* that means parade or drill. This was the parade square of the Jaipur state Army.

Ceremonial occasions saw an impressive gathering of foot soldiers and those astride horses and elephants. State processions that were always watched avidly by the local public left through the Sireh Deori Gate to enter the city streets. It is easy to visualize the magnificent line up of soldiers, nobles and other state dignitaries in all their finery, followed by the Maharaja and his retinue of ministers. The colourful bejewelled turbans, gold inlay work swords, cross belts and long robe like coats... what an imposing sight they must have been! No wonder the local public waited for hours to catch a glimpse of these parades.

When power changed hands and the royal family handed over several of their properties to the state government, **Jaleb Chowk** was one among the many. The state government used it for the local municipal and transport offices. Many have now shifted from here and plans are underway to try and convert this entire area into a tourist complex. For now, it is used mainly to park tourist buses and cars.

GOVINDDEVJI'S TEMPLE

When you have approached almost the centre point of this square take a right turn and go in through a small gate. This will lead you to the oldest part of the City Palace and the structure that Sawai Jai Singh wanted incorporated into the new city – the **Govinddevji Temple**. This temple is dedicated to Lord Krishna, Govind being one of the several names of Lord Krishna and is undoubtedly the most popular temple in Jaipur.

Image of Govinddevji

because it was originally planned as a residence for Sawai Jai Singh, the founder of Jaipur. That is the reason why the structure of this temple is so unlike traditional temples that you may have seen elsewhere. A Hindu temple almost always has a spire, a dome that houses the idol of the god or goddess. This one has a *baradari*, an arched veranda that overlooks a beautifully laid out garden towards the south.

There are tiny shops at the entrance of the temple where flowers and Indian sweets are available on sale for offering to the Lord. The temple is open to all and there is no restriction if you want to offer flowers to the Lord. As you approach the temple, be prepared to go barefeet to enter the main hall. If you want to keep your footwear on, then just turn to the left and walk on the periphery until you get on the front side and have *darshan* from a distance. Many people do so and it is not considered disrespectful.

There is an interesting story behind the temple's foundation.

It is a rare example of a flat roofed Hindu temple but that is

But Jai Singh never did get to stay here. After the structure was completed and Jai Singh was ready to move in, Govinddevji appeared to him in a dream and said that He wanted to reside in the place. Jai Singh immediately changed his

Chandra Mahal view from Govinddevji

plans and moved to Chandra Mahal. There are many temples in the country that have been built in the most unlikely of places and there seems no logical explanation as to their origin and if you try to study their history you will find that more often than not, they are the result of somebody's dream or vision. It is a perfectly acceptable reason.

The image of Govinddevji (Lord Krishna) was brought from Vrindavan and installed here in 1735 as the guardian deity of Jaipur rulers. Then onwards, the maharaja always started his public speeches with 'subjects of Govinda Deva', which implied that they were humble servants of the all-mighty Lord.

The temple has been restored recently and has all manner of decorative elements from gold work on the entire ceiling of the hall, glass chandeliers to murals on the walls.

It is always crowded as devotees sit here chanting *bhajans* (devotional songs) and wait patiently to offer prayers. There are several schedules fixed during the day when the Lord is dressed in different costumes to show different stages of His daily routine. The timings for winter and summer differ and there are seven different *darshans* in a day. The first one is called *Mangala* and the final *darshan* is called *Shayan* after which the *pat*, or doors are closed and the Lord rests for the night.

Jai Niwas gardens

Special religious occasions are celebrated with great pomp and gusto. The best time to visit the temple is during the festival of Holi (March), Janamashtami (July-August) and Annakut, after Diwali (October-November).

Located close to the temple are the **Jai Niwas Garden, Badal Mahal** and **Talkatora** tank.

JAI NIWAS GARDEN

To reach the Jai Niwas Garden, keep walking straight ahead, past the temple and turn right.

Built by Jai Singh II at the same time as the city, this Mughal garden is located just behind Govinddevji temple. This garden was once famous for its meticulous planning and special features like fountains, water channels, and flowerbeds in geometric designs. The Mughals had already introduced Rajputs to some of the most outstanding pavilions, forts and palaces, and their famed gardens. As a result, the Rajputs began to give as much attention to gardens as they did to their palaces. This was the case with Jai Niwas Garden too.

After its construction in the eighteenth century, this garden provided the royal women a beautiful and private area where they could relax and enjoy the scenic beauty. Even today, despite the fountains not working and lack of flowers, this cool, tree-shaded park is a refreshing retreat from the heat and dust of the city.

Badal Mahal

Another dazzling reminder of the past is a hunting pavilion known as **Badal Mahal** that was constructed in 1750 and lies towards the north end of the gardens. The ceilings of this five-arched pavilion are painted in blue and white and traces of the cloud (*badal*) pattern are still visible.

There is not much to see here but it provides some interesting views of the garden and the **Talkatora** tank located below it.

An artificial tank, Talkatora is located to the north of the Jai Niwas Gardens. When constructed, it was surrounded on three sides by a lake,

popularly called **Rajamal ka Talab**, making the smaller tank look like a *tal-ḳatora* or "bowl in a lake". Sawai Jai Singh was quite fond of this rather secluded spot and bred crocodiles here. On special occasions, crocodile shows were also organised for the public. In the later years, the lake around Talkatora was filled in and modern houses used up all the open space.

Over the years, with acute water shortage and indifferent monsoons this is more of a sandy playground than a water reservoir. But its design and placing is interesting. This is the spot where

Badal Mahal

the processions of **Teej** and **Gangaur** culminate.

From the Badal Mahal, come back and turn right in the opposite direction, towards the west and you will find a smaller gate called **Chhattar ki Aad**. Leave the garden through this gate and turn left. Keep going on this road past the shops and take a right turn just before you see an old ruined gateway up ahead, turn left from the huge tree-enclosed temple and keep on this road until it gets you to the **Chaugan Stadium**.

On your left, if you look up you will see sections of the City Palace. They look very close but are not accessible from this side. One very interesting dome, or *chhatri*, is the **Chini ki Burj** that literally means Chinese Dome. Stop and look at the beautiful blue Chinese tiles on the pillars and ceiling of the dome. Most of it has fallen apart but there is enough to give you an idea of the kind of craftsmanship that existed

Chhattar ki Aad

here in the eighteenth century. This is the oldest example of Chinese tiles to be found in the city.

Stay on the right of this road with the **Chini ki Burj** behind you and you will soon come to an open area that is known as **Chaugan Stadium**.

CHAUGAN STADIUM

Chaugan is a Persian word that meant both a curved stick as well as a game played with these sticks, an older version of polo. Over the years, it has come to mean an open place for sports. Originally, this was a heavily fortified large area with several enclosures, pavilions known as *burj*, for the maharaja and his entourage. **Chini ki Burj** was the most notable one of them. Modern buildings have engulfed the other two known as **Moti Burj** and **Shyam Burj**.

During the early days, horses were exercised here and people also gathered to watch lion, wild bull and elephant fights. The common spectators occupied the area close to the ground.

Today, this place comes alive on occasions like **Teej, Gangaur** and the **Elephant Festival**. For the rest of the year, its use is restricted to sports activities like cricket matches and coaching camps for the people in the vicinity and other local gatherings.

opp. Elephant Festival.
Chini ki Burj, Chaugan.

elephants. Dozens of elephants in their best finery participate in various activities like elephant polo and race that are an attraction for tourists as well as the local people.

Your walk ends here and there is a wide road to the west of Chaugan that will take you to

ELEPHANT FESTIVAL

One of the most colourful and eagerly awaited events is the annual **Elephant Festival** held on the day of Holi, the festival of colours. It is a magnificent spectacle that unveils the majesty and grandeur of

Gangauri Bazaar. You can get a scooter rickshaw here to take you back to Jaleb Chowk or your hotel.

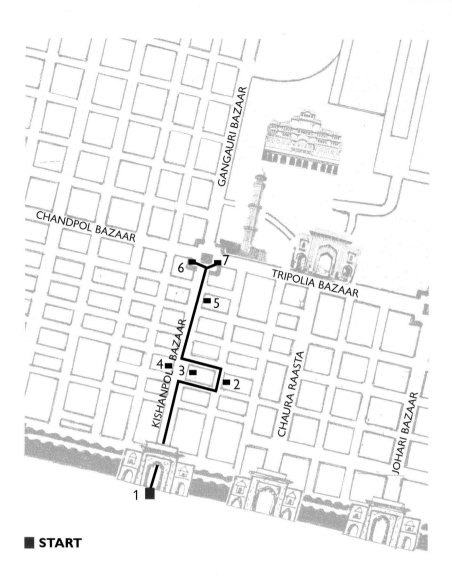

■ **START**

WALK 3

1. Kishanpol Gate
2. Jain Temple
3. Maharaja Arts College
4. Harsh Behari Temple
5. Bhagat Mishtan Bhandar
6. Maharaja Girls High School/Nataniyon ki Haveli
7. Choti Chaupad

WALK 3

KISHANPOL — CHOTI CHAUPAD

Painted temples, uniform shops and some original havelies that haven't been tampered with make this an interesting area to walk in. This walk allows you to see a bit of the inner section of the city to observe the layout of the residential blocks. A good place if you want to shop for some silver.

PARKING

There is ample parking available here. Leave your taxi outside **Kishanpol Gate,** better known as **Ajmeri Gate.** Fortunately, the gates have been so designed that there is a lot of open area on either side of the gate. You could take a scooter/cycle rickshaw back from Choti Chaupad or get your taxi to meet you there.

PLACES OF INTEREST

Ajmeri Gate – Kishan Pol Bazaar – Sanghon ka Raasta – Maharaja College of Arts – Ajaibghar ka Raasta – Chokri Modikhana – Digambar Jain Temple – Harsh Behari ka Mandir – Bhagat Mishthan Bhandar – Maharaja Girls School – Kotwali – Shri Sitaramji ka Mandir – Choti Chaupad

THE WALK

Kishanpol is the first gate located on the south side of the city wall and the first major road that cuts across the main street of the city – the one that runs from east **(Chandpol Gate)** to west **(Surajpol Gate).**

All the gates are pink in colour and similar in design. There are two smaller openings flanking the

on this road that is a new addition but it is easy to cross over to the other side when you want to do so. There is a lot of crisscross that you will need to do because there are interesting things to see and do on both sides of the road.

This was one of the four originally planned markets in the walled city, the other three being **Johari Bazaar, Sireh Deori Bazaar** and **Gangauri Bazaar**. Notice the uniformity in shape and size of the shops lining both sides of the 108 ft wide street. The shops are also conveniently numbered. There are some incongruous structures that have come up that do mar the beauty of the original façade but you can still see several houses that have not changed over the years.

bigger one in the centre. The top portion has domed and pillared pavilions and a parapet with loopholes for musketry.

Walk in through the gate and head northwards. There is a divider

Ajmeri Gate

The shops here sell all manner of goods. The first few are mainly those selling *ayurvedic* and allopathic medicines, general stores to cater to the residential areas located behind the market followed by a large number of cycle shops. This market also comes more alive in the month of January during the kite festival held on **Makar Sankranti** when a lot of temporary kite shops come up here. Making kites and the different strings that go with it, the plain *sadda* and the glass-coated *manja* is an intricate art in itself. It needs a little practise to get these colourful kites in the air but if you want to try your hand

at it, go right ahead and ask any passing youngster to help and he will do so very happily.

MAKAR SANKRANTI
(JANUARY 14)

This annual kite flying festival is held on 14th January, Makar Sankranti according to the Indian calendar. The is the day when the sun enters the northern hemisphere from the southern and is considered a very auspicious day for Hindus. This day is marked by visits to the temple and other religious activities. Temporary kite

Kites on display, during Sankrant

shops spring up all over the city markets. People here are known for their expertise in kite flying and this activity is taken very seriously by the young and the old, sometimes leading to unpleasant brawls over kites. There are contests and one is considered victorious if one is able to bring down the opponent's kite.

The phenomenon starts well before the day of Makar Sakranti as kites make their appearance weeks ahead – and continue weeks after the festival. But on 14th January, it is a treat to watch the skyline of the Pink City. This is the time when you will be tempted to look up as you walk but do keep your eyes on the road because boys tend to spring out of almost nowhere as they go running in the streets with long poles trying to capture kites. Hundreds of kites in the sky, kite flyers on terraces, loud music blaring from almost every rooftop… it is a crazy time, but full of fun as the entire city seems to be in a festive mood.

It is truly an unforgettable experience.

It is interesting to note that the craft of **blue pottery** in Jaipur is very closely linked to that of kite flying. In the days of Maharaja Ram Singh II, there was a royal kite-flying department that organised kite fights. During one such contest, two young potters from Achnera, near Agra, were among the participants. Try as the royal kite flyers did, they could not bring down the kites of these simple potters. After the fight was over, Ram Singh called the potters and congratulated them. He also wanted to know how they were able

to cut across the superior royal strings. Kalu and Churaman, the potters, explained that they had coated their strings with powdered glass that they used in their pottery. Ram Singh immediately invited them to move to Jaipur and teach the local potters this new skill.

Maharani Gayatri Devi

The potters shifted here and blue pottery became an integral part of Jaipur. This art, all but vanished at the start of this century but was revived by the tireless efforts of Maharani Gayatri Devi and continues to flourish to this day.

SANGHON (OR SANGHAKON) KA RAASTA

If you are walking on the left side, cross over when you see shop number 266 on the right. There is a narrow lane just after this shop called **Sanghon Ka Raasta**. It is tiny and crowded so look out for scooters and rickshaws driving at a far greater speed than they should. Go into it and keep walking straight until you get to a large open area. The *chowk*, courtyard, was originally planned as a community space between a block of houses but is used as a car park by the people living there. You needn't go into the parking lot. Turn immediately on your right and you will find a **Digambar Jain** temple built in 1788, the entrance to which is almost concealed behind the shutters of some shops. Walk up the steps and you will see beautiful murals on the wall.

Before you come down the steps, look across the temple and

Detail in Jain temple

Jain Temple

on the other side is a beautifully painted entrance to an old haveli, two floors of which have been thoroughly modernised. There is an equal mix of traditional and modern in this block.

Come down from the temple and walk left on the **Maniharon ka Raasta**. The lane is narrow and a little crowded but interesting because you will see many havelies with some quaint little windows, painted entrances and stained glass ventilators. This diversion will also give you an idea of how the streets and residential houses were planned. As you walk in, you find yourself looking at blocks of houses with just a tiny decorative opening into the street. In some of the fancier houses there are carved balconies, pillars, painted walls and other decorative features but there is not much indication as to what

Entrance to Maniharon ka Raasta

Kala Bhawan

the inner portion is like. In fact, that is the beauty and ingenuity of the design.

Houses in the city were so designed as to be compatible to the climatic as well as social conditions. The buildings always covered the entire plot of land and opened into central courtyards. Normally there were two courtyards; one for use by the male members of the family and their guests and the inner courtyard was for the exclusive use of women. The nobles and important ministers tried to copy the design of their maharaja's palace and sometimes their houses had as many as seven courtyards.

The most interesting and well-maintained haveli here, on the left, is the **Kala Bhawan** with its painted green exterior and two old lampposts. Maharaja Ram Singh II installed these lampposts on the city streets in 1838 at the cost of rupees twenty-five each. There are very few of these lampposts left in the city now. Go past this haveli and take the first turn left.

This is the **Ajaibghar ka Raasta**. Keep on this lane until you come out into Kishanpol Bazaar again. Just before you turn right to reach the Maharaja Art College, you will see a pavement stall where *chapatis* and vegetables are being cooked on the roadside. What is special about this place is that sixty-five year old Nomi Devi Kalal has been running it for the past thirty years and provides two *chapatis* and two vegetable curries for as little as rupees two.

Entrance to Ajaibghar ka Raasta

Rajasthan School of Art

As you come back to Kishanpol Bazaar, the huge corner building on your left is the Rajasthan School of Art also known as **Maharaja Art College**. It was originally built as a residence for Pandit Shiv Deen, prime minister during the time of Ram Singh II, but unfortunately he did not live long enough to enjoy this palatial haveli. It was converted into an art college in 1866. It is one of the several educational, cultural and welfare institutions founded by Ram Singh II. Go into the college by all means if you want to have a closer look.

From the college, look straight ahead on the other side of the road at the temple called **Harsh Behari**

ka Mandir. Cross over for a closer look at the temple that still has a few traces of decorative finishing. Though in a sad state of disrepair at least the original structure has not been tampered with.

Now keep on this side of the road and look up on both sides and you will see quite a few of the original structures holding their own against modern buildings of steel and glass. Look out for two old structures on the right above shop numbers 294-293 (the shop numbers are in decreasing order). A little ahead, on the same side is shop no 261, an old antique shop established in AD 1860. Other interesting old structures to look out for (on the right side) are above shop numbers 243-240 and 200 to 194. On the left side, the building above shop number 105-106 is worth a closer look.

As you approach the end of this road, you'll see more shops dealing with jute, bamboo, straw and a local grass called *sun*. Sacks, brooms, ladders, ropes and hemp strings, cots, baskets and steel furniture seem to spill out on the roads.

Another interesting item you can see here is an indigenous brush – *kutchi* that is used for white wash. This jute brush is still widely used despite all manner of modern brushes now available in the market. There is a great demand for these *kutchis* and *kali* (lime) before the festival of **Diwali**. Traditionally, people clean and white wash their homes just before this festival of lights and generally wait for this time of the year to buy new things for the house.

By now, one is nearly at the end of Kishanpol Bazaar. Just before you reach **Choti Chaupad** look for **Bhagat Misthan Bhandar**, shop number 185 on the right side of the road. This shop has been selling the most delicious *laddoos* and *balushahi* for several years. They are cooked in pure ghee (clarified butter) and lethal for calorie watchers. But try one anyway!

Come back on the left side again as you are about to enter one of the most beautiful buildings not

Ladoos

only on this street but also in Jaipur – the Maharaja Girls High School, originally the **Nataniyon ki Haveli**. Noon Karan Natani was a rich banker who owned property all over town. This haveli is also known as the *saat chowk ki haveli* or the haveli with seven courtyards. Part of this haveli has been converted into a police station.

Carved balconies with intricate *jaali* (lattice) work make this an outstanding example of the capabilities and architectural skills of the Jaipur builders. You can go in if you want but the exterior is far more interesting.

The sheer size of this building will astonish you. To see the other part of the haveli, keep to the side of the school building, past the silver shops and you will come to one of the prettiest police stations you will ever see – the Kotwali! Go past this police station until you reach the steps of the **Shri Sitaramji** temple. Climb up and take a look at the temple interiors as well as the surrounding areas. It is a popular viewing place as it provides some very good views of the city, as well as Nahargarh in the background. One interesting feature of these

Choti Chaupad

chaupads is the fact that there are huge temples placed on all sides of the square.

The chaupad that you are looking down is the first major intersection on the Chandpol – Surajpol Street. Come down the steps and immediately on the left is Vijay Stores (number 245-246) a popular shop that sells diet friendly roasted stuff that you can pick up. It is safe and totally fat free.

CHOTI CHAUPAD

Choti Chaupad was originally called **Amber ki Chaupad** and served as one of the two main squares for public gatherings. In fact, you can see its use even today as people sit in this area chatting and generally doing what is known as "time pass".

This intersection joins four important roads – Chandpol Bazaar to the west, Gangauri Bazaar to the north, Tripolia Bazaar to the east and Kishanpol Bazaar to the south.

Come back towards the **Kotwali**, (police station), go past it and cross the road. This is the end of Kishanpol Bazaar on the right of Choti Chaupad.

The walk ends here and you can find a scooter/cycle rickshaw to take you back or you can explore the Chaupad some more if you want. There are a lot of interesting silver shops here where you can pick up inexpensive gifts and mementoes.

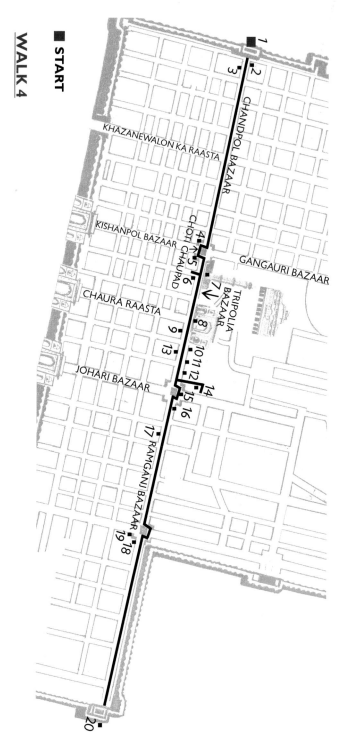

■ **START**

WALK 4

1. Chandpol Gate
2. Hanuman Temple
3. Shri Ramchandraji Temple
4. Shri Chaturbhujji Temple
5. Flower Market

6. Maniharon ka Raasta
7. Isar Lat
8. Tripolia Gate
9. Nawab Saheb ki Haveli
10. Nawal Beharji Temple

11. Shri Chandra Manoharji Temple
12. Brajraj Behari Temple
13. Ramchandra Kuffiwala
14. Hawa Mahal
15. Badi Chaupad

16. Shri Chandra Beharji Temple
17. Islami Kallu Hotel
18. Shri Murli Manoharji Temple
19. Rajputana Haveli
20. Surajpol Gate

WALK 4

CHANDPOL GATE — SURAJPOL GATE

This is the **Rajpath** of Jaipur, the main street that connects the city from the western most point to the one on the east. Originally, it was a 110 ft wide road and has remained so to this day. Four important roads cut across it at right angles. This is the only straight road in the city that can take you in from one gate and out through another without any twists or turns.

Shops, temples, havelies, brass, copper and steel utensils… they are all here on this main shopping lane of yesteryears. If you want to see the markets at their busiest, then this walk is best done during mid morning or late afternoon.

PARKING

You will have to get your car/ scooter rickshaw to drop you off just outside the Chandpol Gate. The place is always busy with countless mini-buses, camel carts and others waiting to push their way in to the market through the rather narrow side gate. You need to be very careful here. Do not bother to stand and admire the structure, it is like the others, just look out for a gap and walk in through the gate quickly. Your taxi can meet you at the Surajpol Gate.

PLACES OF INTEREST

Chandpol Gate – Hanumanji Mandir – Shri Ramchandraji ka Mandir – Choti Chaupad – Flower Market – Isar Lat – Tripolia Bazar – Maniharon ka Raasta –Tripolia Gate – Nawab Saheb Ki Haveli – Badi Chaupad – Mandir on Badi Chaupad – Silver shops – Ismail Kallu Hotel – Ramganj Chaupar – Rajputana Haveli – Surajpol Gate

THE WALK

The walk will take you into the walled city through the Chandpol Gate. This is one of the original seven gates enclosing the walled city. The lane is a little crowded and you will have to jostle for space but it widens very soon as you enter the Chandpol Bazaar. Adjoining the gate, on the left is a very famous Hanuman temple known as the **Chandpol ke Balaji** that is as old

Chandpol gate

as the city itself. Tuesdays and Saturdays are special days and attract more devotees than you would see on other days of the week.

The rulers of Jaipur placed temples at all vantage points, especially near the main entry gates into the city. When the city was planned, there were over four hundred temples constructed in the walled city.

Keep going straight on this street and you will find yourself in a market full of uniform shops that dot both sides of the road. All products ranging from grains to garments, spices to soaps can be found here. Some twenty shops later, on the right hand side, is a huge temple by the name of **Shri Ramchandraji ka Mandir** that was constructed by Maharaja Madho Singh II. On the left when you see shop number 19, cross over, there

Detail from Ramchandraji ka Mandir

Detail from Ramchandraji ka Mandir

you can observe are above shop numbers 118-119, 185 and 192 on the left; and above shop numbers 344-348, 315, 303 on the right.

Just as you reach almost the end of the road, you will see steps going up to a temple, between shop numbers 271-270, known as the **Chaturbhujji ka Mandir** on the right. Cross over and stay on this side.

Shri Chaturbhujji temple

is a gap between the divider. The way to the temple is between shop numbers 445-446. It is one of the most important temples on this road and the sheer size and planning is impressive. Beautifully carved pillars and paintings at the entrance gate lead to one courtyard and then another that houses the idol of Lord Ram. There is a carved silver plated gate and beautiful gold work paintings on either side of the door.

Come back to the left and keep going straight on this side. There are several interesting old buildings and temples on this road and you can cross over to the other side if something unusual catches your eye. Some of the old buildings that

Very soon you will reach a square, this is the first intersection known as **Choti Chaupad.**

CHOTI CHAUPAD

Choti Chaupad is a busy intersection with temples on all sides. The road on the left is **Gangauri Bazaar**, the one going westwards, on the right is the **Kishanpol Bazaar** and the one straight ahead leads you to **Tripolia**

Flower market

Bazaar. It is easier to keep on the right and cross over from the Kishanpol Bazaar side. You will find yourself in a very interesting flower market. This market comes alive in the mornings when farmers bring in their flowers – Indian roses, marigolds and other local varieties tied in wet sacks. Let the sheer colour and pleasant scents permeate your senses. You can pick up a few strands of the sweet scented *mogra* flower and wrap them around your wrist or wear them around the neck. You will love the scents as you move along.

Walk along the single row of flower sellers, as colourfully dressed as their flowers. At the end of the flower market, turn right and go on to the **Tripolia Bazaar**. Also look out for Raja Udai Singh's haveli at the beginning of this street.

TRIPOLIA BAZAAR

Tripolia Bazaar is totally different in the kind of goods that you can get here as also the shoppers who come to this market. One thing that you will notice immediately is the number of utensil shops here that deal mainly in brass, steel, lead, copper and tin utensils as well as gardening and farming implements. You will also find masons looking for the tools of their trade. The first few shops on the left are no less interesting as they deal with costumes for theatre and all manner of props. Things like fake crowns, swords, moustaches and so on are much in demand.

As you walk along Tripolia Bazaar, you will notice two small temples in the middle of the road.

Paper products on sale in Tripolia Bazaar

View from Nawab Saheb ki Haveli

Immediately after the second temple, you will find an arched entrance on the right, after shop number 350. This is the **Maniharon ka Raasta.**

MANIHARON KA RAASTA

Walk into this lane, if only a short distance, to see the famous lacquer artisans at work. Tiny shops dot the narrow lane and you can see women working deftly to shape *lac* bangles. The bright coloured lacquer is gently moulded into shape over burning charcoals, then embedded with fine glass pieces or embellished with gold threads.

Lac is a substance collected from trees and heated and moulded to give it desired forms. Besides bangles, there are pens, key chains, jewellery boxes, small animal statues, figures, *sindoor dani, agarbati* stands, show pieces etc. made of lac. These bangles cost just a few rupees but make an excellent gift.

Hardware shop in Tripolia Bazaar

Come out on the main street again but there is no need to cross over. Keep to the right side and go slowly here until you reach an interesting book-cum-holy picture shop that is set up on the steps of a temple. Make your way past these books and climb to the **Shri Radha Krishnaji's** temple. There is a huge open courtyard with the priest's family staying in a section of the temple. This temple is interesting to see if only to understand how changing times have necessitated the reuse of these spaces.

Come back down and look across the road at the huge tower

Bangle maker, Maniharon ka Raasta

on the left side of the street jutting out from behind the shops. That is the famous **Swarga Suli** or **Isar Lat**.

SWARGA SULI (ISAR LAT)

The tower dominates this side of the market. Maharaja Ishwari Singh built it in AD 1749 to commemorate a grand victory. There is another popular story attached to this structure. It is said

Isar Lat

that Ishwari Singh made it with the sole purpose of looking at the beautiful daughter of his Prime Minister Hargobind Natani who lived in a haveli opposite the Swarga Suli. Protocol did not allow him to go to her house and he was so enamoured with her that he would spend hours looking at her secretly from the tower.

Keep walking straight on this road. Further ahead on the left is the impressive Tripolia Gate. You cannot miss it because it is the next large structure after the Isar Lat. This gate overlooks one of the busiest streets of the walled city called **Chaura Raasta**. The market on either side of the Gate is known as Tripolia Bazaar. It is again a crowded, noisy and interesting area.

TRIPOLIA GATE

Tripolia means three gates. It was constructed in 1734, at the same time as the seven-storey Chandra Mahal. It is a gate with pretty balconies enclosed by *jaalis* at the top end. You will have noticed these pretty *jaali* screens on several

Gangaur procession going past Tripolia Gate

important buildings. They were not there for purely decorative purposes; they had a very important function – to allow ladies to watch the processions, street scenes without being seen. These latticed balconies were for the exclusive use of royal ladies.

Walk past the gate and keep going straight. You are still in Tripolia Bazaar, heading towards Badi Chaupad with many interesting things to see on the way.

NAWAB SAHEB KI HAVELI

Located a short distance from the Tripolia Gate, on the right side of the street, towards the east is the well-maintained eighteenth century **Nawab Saheb Ki Haveli** that stretches over shops 256 to 270. Though named after Nawab Faiz Ali Khan, a prime minister at the time of Maharaja Madho Singh, this haveli had several illustrious occupants. Vidyadhar Bhattacharya was the original owner who lived here to keep an eye on the construction of the new

View from Nawab Saheb ki Haveli

city; **Ras Kapoor**, the infamous courtesan became the next occupant when the haveli was gifted to her by Maharaja Jagat Singh; Nawab Faiz Ali was the last occupant and a great favourite of the maharaja so much so that when the nawab's wife died, Maharaja Madho Singh sent one of the most beautiful courtesans of that time, **Gohar Jan,** to help him through his time of sorrow. Gohar Jan spent many an evening in this haveli and several times the nawab himself went over to her huge haveli in his four-horse driven buggy.

The terrace of this haveli is open to tourists and presents some spectacular views of Jaipur's main streets. A lane named after

Vidyadhar is located after Nawab Sahab ki Haveli.

Directly opposite this haveli, between shops 114 and 115 is **Nawal Behariji's temple** with a decorated doorway and a courtyard with marble pillars.

Gohar Jan, the beautiful courtesan

Bahi Khata shop

You will find a lot of shops selling paper products on the right side of the street. Other than an assortment of items like plates, cups, notebooks, streamers, caps, files and folders, look out for shops (there are several) that can give you the typically Indian notebook called *bahi*. A majority of businessmen in the city still prefer to maintain their accounts in these *bahi khatas*. No fancy computers for them! It is a tradition that has been handed down generation after generation. Another charming tradition that has survived and is still visible in some shops is the preference for floor seating. There are no counters, no chairs, just thick mattresses covered with white sheets. Enter any of these shops and request the shopkeeper, most probably an old timer clad smartly in a spotless white shirt, dhoti and saffron turban, to show you how they maintain their accounts in a *bahi khata*. Smaller *bahis*, red cloth bound and stitched, are available for sale. Good to give as gifts or to write notes.

As you walk on the left side of the street, turn in after shop no.131 and you will find another beautiful temple, that of **Shri Chandra Manoharji,** better known as the temple of Neelmaniji. This temple has two courtyards and the gateway to the inner courtyard has beautiful carvings, marble pillars and paintings.

Pakodi wala outside Brajraj Behari temple

There are a lot of interesting temples here and as you walk past the utensil shops, there is an opening after shop number 162 that leads to a temple dedicated to Lord Krishna called **Shri Brajraj Behari**. This temple has huge courtyards, carved marble pillars and beautifully painted interiors. When you come out there is a tiny shop on the left, shop number 162a, **Haridas Gokulchand Pakodi Wala**, which is famous for its fried lentil *pakodas* (dumplings). If you have a sweet tooth, cross over to the right and look for **Ramchandra Kulfiwala** (shop number 222).

You are now approaching the **Badi Chaupad**. After Choti Chaupad, this is the other important cross section. Just before the intersection, after shop number 179, there is a turning on the left with a policeman directing the traffic. Walk in through this arched entrance; it will lead you to the **Hawa Mahal**. The police headquarters are also located inside this complex and hence, the presence of the traffic policeman.

HAWA MAHAL

This is without doubt Jaipur's best-known monument. It was

Hawa Mahal

Detail, Hawa Mahal

built in 1799 by Sawai Pratap Singh and designed by Lalchand Usta. If you view it from a distance, it looks like a palace with the promise of big, spacious rooms inside. But on closer inspection, you realise that it is little more than a finely chiselled façade. Out of its five floors, the top three are just a room deep while the lower floors are connected to rooms and courtyards. The Hawa Mahal is an enormous tapering structure with numerous arches, spires and a mind-boggling 953 latticed casements and small windows.

It was designed for a single purpose, to allow the women of the royal harem to watch processions that passed through the streets of Jaipur and also people in the city going about their daily business.

Sitting in the cool, airy interior of the Hawa Mahal, they could watch the goings-on below while they themselves remained hidden. Underground tunnels connected the palace to the harem. The maharaja also often came here to compose devotional songs to Lord Krishna in the relative seclusion of the place.

Despite the popular belief that the building was made as a viewing gallery, it is said that Sawai Pratap Singh, a poet and a devotee of the Hindu deities Radha and Krishna, had it designed like a *mukut*, a crown and dedicated the monument to Lord Krishna.

There is a small archaeological museum on the same site, with exhibits dating back several centuries.

Come back on Tripolia Bazaar and keep going straight. The intersection up ahead is the second important square after the Choti Chaupad.

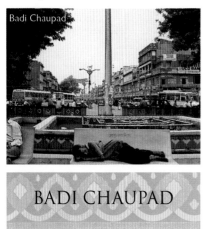
Badi Chaupad

BADI CHAUPAD

You may like to explore **Badi Chaupad** a bit before continuing to **Ramganj Bazaar**. At the end of Tripolia Bazaar, on your immediate left, is an interesting little temporary market (though it has been there for a few decades) that caters to women and has anything from bangles to ribbons and other trinkets. Walk through it, even though it is narrow, lined with very small shops. The area is lively and fascinating.

If you're looking at Badi Chaupad with Tripolia Bazaar behind you, then to the left of Badi Chaupad is **Sireh Deori Bazaar**, to the right is **Johari Bazaar** and straight ahead is **Ramganj Bazaar**. When you come out of this temporary market, it will get you to the start of the Sireh Deori Bazaar. It is easier to cross from this end of the Chaupad. On the other side is the **Shri Chandrabehariji** temple. It is partly concealed by a huge tree in front of the entrance but it is worth the climb. Placed next to it is another police station called the **Manak Chowk Thana,** an imposing building that was originally a temple. The entrance to the temple is from the side.

There are some interesting shops near the police station and a corner shops sells very good *ittar* or Indian perfume. Ask for popular fragrances like *khas, gulab* and *kevada*. You can get a sampling in a small piece of cotton wool dipped in the strong perfume.

Turn left onto the main Ramganj Bazaar now.

RAMGANJ BAZAAR

This walk is a shopper's delight as it takes you near the famed lanes where the craftsmen live and practise crafts that have been handed down to them by their ancestors and mentors. This area has a predominantly Muslim population and the lanes and by lanes of this section are chock-a-block with artists, miniature painters, silver foil makers, printers, dyers, leather shoe and saddle makers, dyers, brass inlay workers and woodcrafters. In fact, some of the city's best artists live here. This place is good for leather, silver and antiques and good bargains are available here.

After Chandpol Bazaar and Tripolia Bazaar, this bazaar will seem more congested and walking on the pavement is not always possible here because they are lined with temporary stalls.

There are two mosques on the right of the road and nestled

Miniature artist

between them is a popular restaurant called **Islami Kallu Hotel**. Notice the crowd sitting just outside the hotel waiting for a free meal. The owner has been distributing free meals to the less privileged from the time he set up the restaurant.

The interesting buildings are scattered on both sides of the street and are generally double storied. Located above the shops on the left is Ladliji ka Mandir, a temple dedicated to Radha, the consort of Lord Krishna. There is another imposing structure, half of which is a temple and half a dispensary. It is almost always closed so you can admire the building from across the road.

Tie and Dye process

Brass inlay worker

If you look at the building above the shops, you will notice another interesting feature – there are more residences here than commercial buildings. Some are new and some dilapidated and some original houses with their tin projections, arched windows and salmon pink colour.

The by-lanes are very interesting but not recommended for the lone walker. It is best to stay on the main Ramganj Bazaar.

Jooti maker

Though a very busy and old area, there is not much in this market that would bring regular shoppers here so development has not been as fast paced in Ramganj as in other parts of the walled city.

As you walk on this road, you will get to the **Ramganj Chaupad**.

RAMGANJ CHAUPAD

With Ramganj behind you, the road on the left, going northwards is the **Ghoda Nikas Road**, straight ahead is the **Surajpol Bazaar** and the road on the right is the **Ghat Darwaja Bazaar**. After having seen the other two **chaupads** you will note some basic similarities in the layout, the placing of temples on the corners, the four wide streets leading from it but the similarities end here. When the *chaupads* were planned, **Ramganj Chaupad** was just as important as the other two but over the years its importance has diminished drastically. Development seems to have passed it by. After you have explored the surroundings, the next thing that will hit you is the hundreds of cycle rickshaws that are parked all around the *chaupad*. Nowhere else in the city will you see so many of them parked in one place.

On the left of the Chaupad, before you cross over is the house of the famous courtesan **Gohar Jan.** Just see it from the outside. A government dispensary occupies it now but at one time it played host to prime ministers and other important guests from the state. Jaipur had a tradition of these *tawaifs* who were cultured, sang beautifully and were considered artists in their own right.

Two buildings of some interest are a huge temple dedicated to **Shri Murlimanoharji** on the right of this *chaupad* and adjoining it a huge and impressive haveli called the **Rajputana Haveli**. This haveli has

been the subject of many an architect's study. The family is quite open to having visitors dropping in so if you wish to have a closer look you may walk in. The name and telephone number of the haveli is very conveniently painted on the outside wall.

The road proceeds straight to go on to Suraj Pol, the eastern end of the city. It is a wide road, easy to walk on and not as crowded as the other areas. There are several old structures, much smaller in size than the ones you may have seen in the other areas but interesting in their own way. As mentioned earlier, **Chowkri Topkhana Hazuri** was one of the least developed areas and never designed as a planned residential section. For several

Temple and dispensary, Ramganj

them, this Chowkri had only twelve thousand.

Walk on until you see the **Surajpol Gate**. Outside the gate and a little further away, you will notice another gate and a hillock behind. That is the **Galta Gate** and not really a part of the walled city.

years, it remained a sandy patch and then grew as a slum populated by labourers from outside the city. There are no fancy havelies, no decorative balconies, no painted entrances and no wide by-lanes, maybe a stray temple here and an odd building there. In the early nineteenth century, when the rest of the *Chowkris* had over twenty thousand people living in *each* of

This is the end of the walk and also the last point of the eastern side of the city. The road outside is fairly busy as it is the Delhi by-pass road. It is possible to get a scooter rickshaw here.

Surajpol Gate

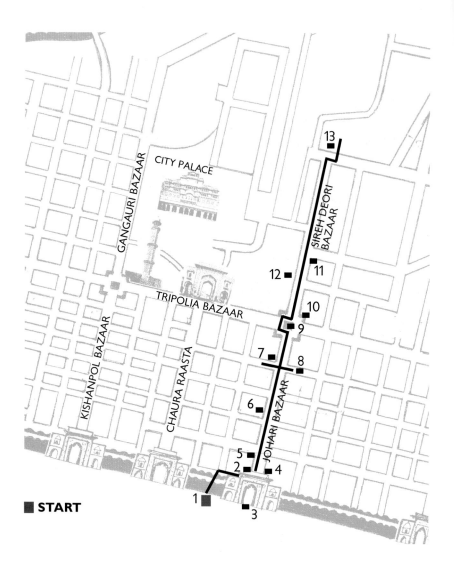

WALK 5

1. Link Road
2. Hanuman Temple
3. Sanganeri Gate
4. Roop Chandramaji Temple
5. Sheesh Mahal of Ras Kapoor
6. Lakshmi Mishtan Bhandar
7. Gopalji ka Raasta
8. Haldiyon ka Raasta
9. Badi Chaupad
10. Maharaja High School
11. Shri Ramchandraji Temple
12. Hawa Mahal
13. Kale Hanumanji Temple

WALK 5

LINK ROAD — KALE HANUMANJI TEMPLE

It is famous, it is crowded, and it is a shopper's delight. Johari Bazaar is your best bet if you are looking for traditional saris and *lehengas* in colourful *lahariya* (stripes) or *bhandhej* (tie and dye) or glittering gemstone jewellery. Traditionally, it was the lane of the jewellers (*johari* means jeweller) but today occupied by an equal number of cloth-merchants.

This is one of the busiest streets in Jaipur but easy to walk on with the newly vacated verandas outside the shops. Minor diversions into the by-lanes can be a rewarding experience.

PARKING

The starting point of this walk is the parking area outside the Ram Niwas Bagh. It is a busy parking space almost always crowded but slightly better in the morning hours. You can get your car or rickshaw to drop you just outside Link Road, a road that connects to **Bapu Bazaar** and meet you at **Kale Hanumanji** temple at **Sireh Deori Bazaar.**

PLACES OF INTEREST

Link Road – Bapu Bazar – Sanganeri Gate – Hanumanji Ka Mandir – Johari Bazaar – Sheesh Mahal of Ras Kapoor – Haldiyon Ka Raasta – Badi Chaupad – Hawa Mahal – Sireh Deori Bazar – Maharaja Boys School – Mandir Shri Ramchandraji – Hawa Mahal – Kale Hanumanji Temple

THE WALK

It is among the newer, modern markets and very busy. This area has been redesigned for the convenience of pedestrians yet one needs to be careful of cycles and scooters. The shops on both sides of this lane seem geared for tourists as you can get readymade garments, Rajasthani *jooties* (shoes), lac and glass bangles, hand block printed bedcovers and table covers, bags and items for the house. It is all there in this market.

At the end of Link Road, is the **Bapu Bazaar**. The small lane right

Bazaar. This has almost the same kind of shops and is largely dominated by garment shops.

If you keep walking on this road it will lead you to the beginning of the famous Johari Bazaar.

Top: Traditional Rajasthani tie and dye saris
Left: The famous Jaipuri Jooties
Below: Handblock printed products

in front of you, across the road is famous for its snacks and savouries. If you are not too fussy about what you eat then do try the *chat pakoris*, especially *gol gappas* or *pani puris*. Turn right to come on to Bapu

SANGANERI GATE

As you approach Johari Bazaar, look on your right to see the **Ram Pol** better known as **Sanganeri Gate** that would lead you out on Mirza Ismail Road, popularly known as M.I. Road. If you want

be explored. You would need to cross over to the right. Be careful as this is the beginning of Johari Bazaar and there is heavy traffic here, going both in and out of Johari Bazaar.

Come back to the left after you have seen the temple and stay on this side. This area has a mix of seed

Sanganeri Gate

to see the front portion of the gate you can take a slight diversion and come back again through the gate. For Johari Bazaar, just turn left. The first monument of importance is a **Hanuman Temple** on your left. On the opposite side is the **Shri Roopchandramaji** temple that can

and fertilizer shops. A few shops later you'll see some fruit shops. Try a glass of fruit juice, it is fresh, and hygienic.

Near the fruit shops is a small lane turning in to the left. Walk in a bit and you will see the coloured glass balcony over a small gateway.

It is in rather bad shape now but will give you an idea where the most powerful woman of her time stayed. This is the remnant of the Sheesh Mahal of the famous and powerful concubine by the name of **Ras Kapoor.**

RAS KAPOOR

As mentioned earlier, Maharaja Pratap Singh was so enamoured of this woman that he wanted all his courtiers to acknowledge her as the maharani of half of Jaipur and give her due respect. This led to a lot of discontent and rebellion within his courtiers and ultimately, this beauty was imprisoned and banished to Nahargarh (known as Sudarshangarh that time).

Come back the way you went in and proceed on this road.

JOHARI BAZAAR

The verandas have recently been vacated after a long and protracted battle with the shop owners and are safe to walk on. There is no fear of being knocked down by speeding traffic. This is how the markets were originally planned. Keep your eyes on the buildings because despite new commercial complexes having come up there are still some original buildings left, like the building located behind shop number 56 on the left.

A little distance away is the famous restaurant called LMB or **Laxmi Mishtan Bhandar,** a very popular sweets shop of Jaipur. Try the *dahi bada, mishri mawa* or *ghewar.*

There are buildings on both sides of the road and as you go along, you will see a huge building

Street façade Johari Bazaar

with **Standard Pharmacy** written on it. It is Deorhiji temple and still retains its original look. On the right again, between shops number 266 and 267 is **Shri Ratan Behariji's** temple. On the left is **Shri Chandrabehariji's** temple.

The best of Rajasthan's rich craft heritage that includes fabulous fabrics in lovely prints, precious and semi-precious stones,

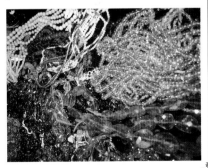

Kundan, Meenakari jewellery, embroidered leather work, other hand crafted items of lac, glass, brass, silver and gold can be found here. The best time to get a feel of this area is during the wedding season when people throng to these shops for trousseau shopping.

When you are getting closer to the **Badi Chaupad**, you will find two lanes on either side. What makes these lanes interesting is the fact that the **Gopalji ka Raasta** on the left is famous for its Indian sweets and jewellery shops. If you want to see the local delicacies being prepared, walk in. Fortunately, these shops are right at the beginning so one needn't go

A sweet shop in Gopalji ka Raasta

by these craftsmen since time immemorial. These jewellers are known the world over for their skills in the craft of **meenakari** and **kundan**.

MEENAKARI

too much into the interior to see the interesting activity of *ladoos* and *jalebies* being made with deft hands. A must see item is the famous *ghewar*, a honeycomb disc shaped sweet fried to a golden brown and dipped in sugar syrup and topped with cream. This is available during the festival of Gangaur and Teej. Hundreds of people wait patiently for their turn to buy these sweets.

The lane on the right is called **Haldiyon ka Raasta** named after a rich banker. **Surana**, the famous jeweller's old haveli-showroom is in this lane. The smaller lanes contain the original jeweller workstations – or *gaddis* – inhabited

Meenakari is known as the setting of precious stones into gold and the enamelling of gold. Raja Man Singh of Amber brought this intricate art to Jaipur when he invited some skilled workers from Lahore. The art has grown over the years and the **meenakari** here is famous for its delicacy and brilliant use of colour.

KUNDAN

This was the form of setting for stones in gold until claw settings were introduced. It is a very tedious process and one that requires a lot of expertise. The pieces are first shaped by specialized craftsmen and soldered together if the shape is complicated. Holes are cut for the stones, any engraving or chasing is carried out, and the pieces are enamelled. When the stones are to be set, *lac* is inserted in the back and is then visible in the front through the holes. Highly refined gold, *kundan*, is then used to cover the *lac* and the stone is pushed into the *kundan*.

Traditional kundan work jewellery

More *kundan* is applied around the edges to strengthen the setting and give it a neat appearance. Several craftsmen are involved in the making of a single piece of jewellery – the *chiterias* make the design, the *ghaarias* the engraving, the *meenakar* is the enameller and the *sunar* is the goldsmith.

After you have explored both these lanes, come back on to Johari Bazaar and keep going straight towards Badi Chaupad. There is an important mosque on the left of the

View of Sireh Deorhi Bazaar from Hawa Mahal

road and just before the mosque, look over shop no.161 and you will see a very interesting façade of a carved exterior. Directly opposite is another building that has retained its original look.

You will now get to **Badi Chaupad** that was designed as an important cross-section and it still continues to hold that place. It is very crowded during peak hours and needs very careful manoeuvring when you cross over to go on to the **Sireh Deori** or Hawa Mahal Bazaar. Keep on the left side, the one that will take you below Hawa Mahal. What you see from the road is merely the back of

the building. This must be the only monument in the world where the rear portion is far better recognised and more famous than the front side!

For photographs, it is better to cross over and get a better view of this monument. Right across from Hawa Mahal, the huge building in the corner is the **Maharaja High School**, one of the many old

Jaipuri quilts

a huge tree, that sell the famed Jaipuri quilt. These quilts are special because they are very light – only five hundred gm of cotton wool is used in the filling.

Some important temples and havelies here are **Bhatt Raja ki Haveli, Vidhayak Niwas, Kalki temple, Dhabhai ji ki Haveli** and **Shri Goverdhan Nathji** temple.

Shri Goverdhan Nathji has wide-open courtyards, elegantly carved marble pillars, and a worship hall with immaculate geometrical perfection floral patterns and designs shown in plaster.

structures you will see on this road. This market, **Sireh Deorhi Bazaar** has one of the best skylines in Jaipur.

There are countless shops near Hawa Mahal and on the opposite side that cater to the tourists. Miniature paintings, antique dealers, leather footwear, saddles and other equestrian goods can be purchased here but be prepared to bargain.

Adjoining the Hawa Mahal, the huge block that you see is the **Town Hall**. The old Rajasthan Legislative Assembly building that now lies vacant with its reuse yet to be decided. Directly opposite the Town Hall are several shops, under

Next to it is the **Shri Ram Chandraji** temple that is a fine example of Jaipur architecture. All possible elements of Hindu, Jain, Mughal traditions have been used to adorn its façade and decorate its

interiors. There are numerous *jharokhas*, brackets and *chhajjas*. The design of stone parapets is common in all parts of building. It is certainly worth a closer look.

The office of the **Devasthan Vibhag**, or the department that looks after temples in Rajasthan is also located here if you want more information on the temples that you have visited.

Cross over to the left and you will go past the **Sireh Deori Gate** that leads to the City Palace. Keep walking on this side but look out for the imposing **Khwasji ki haveli** on the right. In fact, there is so much to see here that if you don't look carefully enough you'll miss

some real gems – like the small building next to the huge **Shimla Hotel**. Stop and admire the original iron grills on this building.

On the left is a famous **Pandit Kulfi Bhandar** that sells *kulfi* or Indian ice cream. A little further, also on the left, hidden behind the buses that are parked in front, is the first theatre of Jaipur – the **Ram Prakash Theatre**. Built by Maharaja Ram Singh II, this is now

defunct and awaits revival. It was later converted into a cinema hall and screened movies up to the early eighties. It was better known as *khatmal wala* hall or the bedbug hall because one always came out of the hall scratching wildly!

Keep going straight on this road. It is a little crowded as dozens of mini buses are parked here waiting to pick up passengers. Walk old temple built by **Sawai Jai Singh** in 1740 and has beautiful carved marble pillars and painted interiors. Go straight ahead and you will see the temple of **Shri Girdhariji**. There is a road going all around it, the entrance is on the left. It is a huge complex and parts of it have been put to commercial use but it is worth going in to explore.

Temple of Shri Girdhariji

carefully and cross the road when the main road turns right to go on to Amber through **Zorawar Singh Gate**.

Right in front of you is the sidewall of a temple called **Kale Hanumanji ka Mandir**. This temple is located on the **Girdhariji ke Mandir ka Raasta**. It is a very

The walk ends here. You can walk back to the **Kale Hanumanji** temple and take a scooter rickshaw from here.

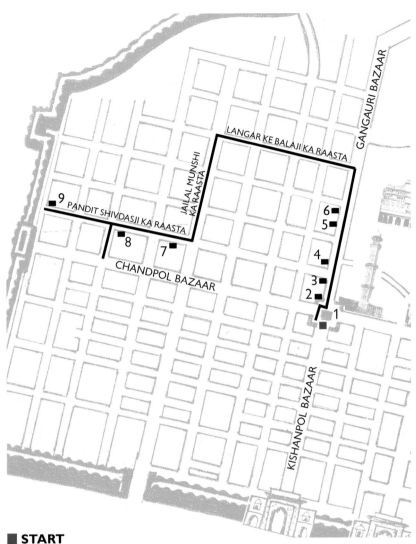

■ **START**

WALK 6

1. Choti Chaupad
2. Shri Chaturbhuj Temple
3. Roop Chaturbhuj Temple
4. Choti Maharaniji ka Nohra

5. Shri Girdhariji Temple
6. Shri Vijay Govindji Temple
7. Shri Gopinathji Temple
8. Khatu House
9. Balanandji's Math

CHOTI CHAUPAD — CHANDPOL BAZAAR

This is one of the most un-spoilt areas of the walled city. No commercial complexes have come up here and the residential use of this **Chowkri Purani Basti** has been maintained. Unlike the other *chowkris*, this one is not as crowded and offers a leisurely walk where one can observe the special features that make Jaipur special. The layout of the streets and the residences, the decorative entrances, the well planned havelies with their courtyards, the tiny windows planned in a way that they kept the harsh sun out and allowed enough light and air to filter in.

PARKING

Gangauri Bazaar is a fairly wide street and parking is available on the left of Choti Chaupad. It is a good idea to have the taxi pick you up at the finishing point near **Chandpol,** just outside **Uniara Raoji ka Raasta.**

PLACES OF INTEREST

Choti Chaupad – Gangauri Bazaar – Langar ke Balaji Ka Raasta – Jailal Munshi ka Raasta – Pandit Shivdasji ka Raasta – Balanandji Ka Math

THE WALK

Choti Chaupad is a busy traffic intersection so cross over to the Gangauri Bazaar side carefully. You will see several fruit and vegetable sellers on the left side. Also on the left side are steps leading to a temple on the top left side with two marble elephants at the entrance. This is the **Shri Chaturbhuj Temple.** You can climb up for a look

Shri Chaturbhuj Temple

at the beautiful frescoes and for another view of the **Chaupad** – this time towards Kishanpol Bazaar to the south.

Keep to the left and walk past the carts of fruit sellers and then down the road that slopes down towards the north – the **Gangauri Bazaar.**

GANGAURI BAZAAR

This road has been named after the famous festival of **Gangaur.** It is the most important local festival celebrated in Jaipur. This spring festival is held in honour of *Gauri*, the goddess of abundance. Girls dress up in their finest clothes and pray for a spouse of their choice, while married ladies do the same for the happiness of their husbands. Although celebrated throughout Rajasthan with great enthusiasm, the celebrations in Jaipur have their own charm and attraction.

Colourful images of **Gauri,** beautifully dressed and bejewelled, are taken out in procession with the town band in attendance. Thousands of people from the countryside come to the city to be a part of the procession. It is a

Flower seller on Choti Chaupad

delightful time to be in Jaipur as you see cheerful men and women in their colourful best out to enjoy every moment of their time away from home: Shopping, eating at roadside stalls and singing folk songs with gay abandon.

The procession in Jaipur starts from the City Palace and passes through Gangauri Bazaar to go on to Chaugan.

The streets here are also lined with uniform shops but what is most interesting here is that there are as many temporary shops on the pavement as there are built shops. Pavement shops seem to dominate this stretch from Choti Chaupad down to Gangauri Bazaar. Men and women can be seen selling mainly vegetables and fruits while behind them are shops selling grain, molasses, cheap furniture made from packing crates and other recycled wood. The Indian easy chair known as *mudha* is also available here. It is a market known for its reasonable rates.

Walk down this street and keep your eyes open because like in the

Teej procession

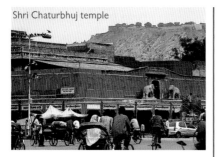
Shri Chaturbhuj temple

other markets, there are still a lot of old buildings that have not been

building here is a temple, among the important ones are on the left **Roop Chaturbhujji** Temple, after shop number 16 and **Shri Girdhariji** temple after shop number 53. Look out for other interesting structures – a beautiful painted doorway after shop number 49, soon after the temples, called **Choti Maharaniji ka Nohra**

tampered with. Painted entrances, carved balconies, all typical of the Jaipur style of architecture can be found here. Almost every other

(it has **Khandelwal Bhawan** written outside it) and **Badi Maharaniji ka Nohra**. Nothing seems to have changed in these buildings over the years and they seem to belong to the eighteenth century, if not earlier. That, in fact, can be said of quite a few buildings on both sides of this road. Do not be in a hurry to walk past the buildings. There is much to see here and enjoy – like the remnant of an iron lamppost just outside shop number 671 on the right. Also,

do not be surprised if some local lads decide to give you an unasked for guided tour. It may just be worth it!

Keep walking straight until you have walked past a gate on your right known as the **Gangauri Gate**. You cannot miss it because it is the only gate on the right and the name is written very clearly on it. This is one very good thing you will find in Jaipur, names are written on the corner of every lane.

On your left, just before a rather wide lane that turns left is **Shri Vijay Govindji's** temple. Walk on the left side of the road until you come to a lane called **Langar ke Balaji ka Raasta.**

This road runs parallel to the Chandpol Bazaar. The entry point seems a little congested but after you have walked for a few yards you will notice that it is quite a wide lane. It will take you past a few small shops, workshops and newly constructed temples. Look on both sides of the road and you will see interesting structures.

After you have walked about half a kilometre, you will see a huge tree right in the middle of the road. Go past this and then take the first

left after the tree. The corner building is also a temple albeit a modern one with another tree growing inside the walled enclosure. This is the **Jailal Munshi ka Raasta.**

JAILAL MUNSHI KA RAASTA

Jailal Munshi was a respected figure in the Maharaja's *darbar* and a lot of lanes in the walled city have been named after important dignitaries working with the Maharajas viz. *Nataniyon Ka*

Old haveli on Jailal Munshi ka Raasta

Raasta, Vidyadhar ka Raasta, Haldiyon ka Raasta, Sanghiji Ka Raasta and so on.

Walk slowly because this is one of the least exploited areas of the walled city. See the havelies, still in very good condition; see the lanes without too much encroachment having marred their beauty. Watch elderly people sitting outside their havelies and chatting or just watching the world go by. There are no speeding scooter or motorcycles trying to push you off the road nor are there any crowds that you need to jostle against. Stop at a temple, and there are several on this road, and look at the beautiful interiors. People are generally quite warm and friendly and will happily give you any information that you need.

This walk will take you to a crossing with **Diwan Shivdasji ka Raasta** cutting across Jailal Munshi ka Raasta. Turn right on this road and you'll find this slightly narrower lane going past some more interesting old havelies.

On the left is **Shri Gopinathji temple.** You cannot miss the extensively painted and arched entrance. **Chowkri Purani Basti** was earmarked for the palatial havelies of the leading courtiers of Jaipur. The havelies of the thakurs (nobles) of Bagru, Uniara, Mahar, etc., are all located in this section.

Shri Gopinathji temple

Care was taken to ensure proper drainage and good lighting. At the time of Maharaja Ram Singh II, a Gas Lighting Department was set up that looked after the upkeep of streetlights. There were cleaners who would start work at very early hours to keep the streets clean and a *bhisthi,* a water carrier, would carry water in a *pakhal,* a treated buffalo skin bag carried on the back with an outlet to sprinkle water, as he moved on the street to settle the dust.

This has remained largely a residential area and there are very few commercial complexes here. Shops do exist but not as many as you would find in some of the other areas. You can walk at a leisurely pace without having to worry too much about traffic. But do look out for stray animals.

Towards the end of this lane you will find **Khatu House** on the left side, the ancestral home of the world-renowned photographer, late Raghubir Singh (whose books *Rajasthan* and *Ganga* had won him world acclaim). It is the corner haveli, just before the **Uniara Raoji ka Raasta**. Don't miss the stone stubs outside this well-preserved haveli that were once used to tie horses.

One of the several palatial havelies of the leading courtiers of Jaipur.

Entrance, Khatu House

Go past Khatu House and up ahead you will see a huge building that seems to dominate the skyline. That is the **Balanandji ka Math**. Just after Khatu House, the road will fork into two. Take the right one and keep on it, it will lead you to the huge complex. Just outside the gate is a dairy – a small hut with some half a dozen buffaloes tied inside.

BALANANDJI KA MATH

The imposing structure that confronts you has a very interesting history behind it. Vrajanand, a recluse was the Jagat Guru, or Universal Teacher of the Ramanuja sect of the Vaishnavas during Jai Singh's time. The maharaja held the guru in great reverence and

became his disciple. He built this Vishnu temple for the *sanyasi*. It is now known as the Balanandji's math because after Vrajanand's death, his disciple Balanandji Maharaj took over the role of guru from his master. He went on to play a very crucial role in providing a defence force to the Jaipur state. The *math* was used as a state military base with several thousand militant Naga sadhus living here. These sadhus proved their mettle against the Mughal armies as well in the battle of Tunga and Bharatpur.

The complex used to be a hub of activity with the militants and their fleet of horses and elephants. These sadhus were respected for

Balanandji ka Math

their valour in battle but their number dwindled drastically and today there are only four sadhus living here. For most of the year, this place is quiet and pretty lifeless but once a year, on the day of Balanandji birth anniversary, hundreds of sadhus gather here to pay homage to their guru.

Come back towards Khatu House and walk out from the **Uniara Raoji ka Raasta** that is the lane adjoining Khatu House. This lane has some other havelies like the Uniara House, Raithal House, Man House, Shahpura House but most of them are either sold or rented out.

One interesting aspect of this lane is that it leads to that section of Chandpol Bazaar where the famous dancing girls, or *tawaifs* used to live. Jaipur used to be the centre of a Rajasthani dance form known as *mujra*. This dance was performed in *kothas* – special havelies belonging to families of the dancers. You will find a lot of black and white picture postcards of the better-known *tawaifs* of Jaipur with antique dealers.

Walk out to the Chandpol Bazaar from where you can get public transport.

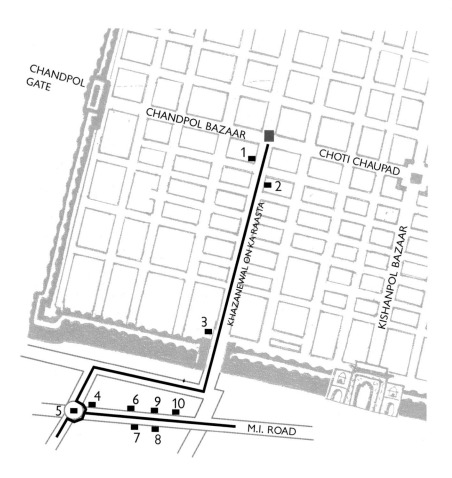

■ START

WALK 7

1. Khazanewalon ki Haveli
2. Ghadi Sazon ki Haveli
3. Singh Dwar
4. Amrapali
5. Panch Batti
6. Lassiwallah
7. Natraj
8. Niros
9. Gem Palace
10. P M Allahbuksh

WALK 7

KHAZANEWALON KA RAASTA — MIRZA ISMAIL ROAD

This is Chowkri Topkhana Desh and the highlight of this walk is **Khazanewalon ka Raasta**, the lane of the marble statue makers. The entire lane is clogged more with tiny shops selling readymade garments than with marble carvers for whom this lane was famous. Yet, there are still quite a few of them working here and the constant noise of stone being hammered and chiselled can be heard at several places. The street takes you out at **Indira Bazaar** and then out of the walled area through **Singh Dwar**, a smaller opening out of the walled city, towards the newer section of the city – the **Mirza Ismail Road**.

DURATION

Although the length of the walk is quite short, there is so much to see, along the route that it may take up to two hours.

PARKING

There is a rather crowded area and you would do better to get dropped right outside **Khazanewalon ka Raasta** and ask your car to meet you on **Mirza Ismail Road** near **Gem Palace** or **Niros**. Taxis and scooter rickshaws are readily available on this road.

PLACES OF INTEREST

Khazanewalon ka Raasta – Indira Bazaar – Singh Dwar – Panch Batti – Mirza Ismail Road

THE WALK

Khazanewalon ka Raasta is a fairly wide lane, fourth on the right when you come in from Chandpol

gate and on the left if you come in from Choti Chaupad. The turning is located between shop number 358 and 359.

KHAZANEWALON KA RAASTA

Khazanewalon ka Raasta

Crowded, busy and very noisy, this street is famous for the marble stone carvers who can be seen chiselling away at huge blocks of marble turning out the most beautiful idols of gods and goddesses as well as politicians. However, when you walk into this lane, it will seem more like a cloth market because there seem to be more readymade garment shops than marble ones.

There are two temples, at the beginning of the lane, on either side dedicated to **Shri Badrinarayan,** the diety of sculptors. A little further into the lane are some old havelies

Marble stone carvers

that go back 250 years but are now either ruined or have been converted into showrooms. Most of them belong to important courtiers of Maharaja Ram Singh's *darbar*.

Do not miss the old houses struggling to stay alive in a street that is fast being changed by modern buildings. A carved balcony here and a painted wall there, a tin shed with designed frill edges – all from the early days.

The first haveli on the right as you enter the lane is of Maharaja Ram Singh's treasurer, Shri Radha Govind Mathur known as **Khazanewalon ki Haveli**. It is in a dilapidated state but still occupied by his descendents.

Another haveli on the left, after the second lane is of **Shri Nandkishore Sharma** known as **Ghadi Sazon ki Haveli** that belonged to a proficient watchmaker in Maharaja Ram Singh's time. It has obviously seen better days and is occupied by the same family. On the same side of the street is another interesting old structure from the olden days, **Mir Munshi ki Haveli**.

As you walk along this crowded lane, you would really have to look out for these old buildings, as they seem to be lost behind dozens of garment shops and their hoardings. This wide lane has narrowed considerably due to shops extending on to the road. A lot of carts and temporary shops usurp a lot of space on the road. But it is easier to walk here than drive! As you go past the clothing shops and have reached almost the middle of this entire lane, you can see a few marble show rooms with the finished product. There are some shops where it is possible to see the work in progress but they are mainly located in the side lanes so do go into these lanes to see these skilled carvers at work.

Rajasthan is a major producer of marble. Statues on religious themes are in great demand.

It is amazing how the skilled craftsman can bring to life intricate details, folds and expressions of personalities in marble sculptures. The tedious and clever workmanship can be visualized when you look at the finished products.

Idols of Lord Krishna, and Lord Ram are the most popular and ordered by temples and individuals from all over the world. In fact, these craftsmen also go out and work on site on bigger pieces. Other than statues, they also specialize in pots, coasters, plates, tiles, paintings, showpieces, animal statuettes, etc. Sometimes enhancing them with subtle use of colour, precious and semi precious gemstones, decorative gold and *meenakari* work is also done. Traditional paintings are also done on marble. There are no further turnings on this lane, except if you need to explore the marble carvers in the by-lanes.

Keep going straight until you get to a wider crossroad – the **Indira Bazaar**. Explore if you must, though the shops here really cater to local needs from shoes to coolers and furnishings. Right in front of you is a small opening that will take you out of the walled city. Known as **Singh Dwar**, it is not one of the original gates of the walled city but something that came up much later for easier access into the crowded market place. Outside Singh Dwar, take a right turn and keep walking parallel to the city wall until you come to a huge banyan tree on your right and the road takes a left turn.

This road will bring you to **Panch Batti**, or Five Lights, a popular crossing on **Mirza Ismail Road**. This has identical cream colour buildings overlooking it. On the left corner is a very famous silver jewellery showroom called **Amrapali**. This has the most

Tribal silver jewellery

gorgeous collection of silver tribal jewellery as well as antiques. Amrapali is one of the pioneers in marketing tribal silver jewellery in the west and very popular with buyers. Some of the traditional ornaments are *hasli, rakhri, timaniyan, bala, bajuband, gajra,*

gokhru, jod, etc. Tribal women wear heavy, simply crafted old silver or ivory jewellery that weighs up to five kilograms. Enduring quality, intricate designs, fine craftsmanship and subtle use of precious and semi precious stones makes Jaipur jewellery especially attractive to buyers.

If you are not too tired, then go straight and you will find **MacDonald's** on your left and then one of Jaipur's smarter cinema halls called **Raj Mandir**. Opposite the Raj Mandir is **Barista**, a good place for coffee and a light snack.

Come back the same way and turn right on Mirza Ismail Road.

MIRZA ISMAIL ROAD, PANCH BATTI

Mirza Ismail Road, or M.I.Road, is named after one of Jaipur's most famous prime ministers, **Sir Mirza Ismail**. This wide road runs parallel to the south-facing wall of the city and a major shopping centre that has several famous jewellery and readymade garments showrooms. Though efforts have been made to maintain some kind of uniformity in the façade here, it hasn't really been possible because this is comparatively a new area. There are some very modern looking buildings on this road.

Some of the city's best restaurants are also located on this road. Five minutes from Panch

Surya Mahal

Batti is the famous *lassiwallah* listed in almost all good city guide-books. Don't get confused when you see four other *lassiwallahs* claiming to be 'original'. The first one on the

A traditional thali

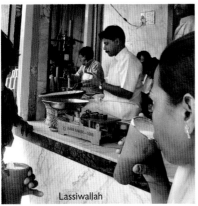
Lassiwallah

left, **Kishanlal Govind Narayan Agarwal** is the oldest one who has been giving the most heavenly *lassi* in earthen cups since 1944.

This is the end of the walk now and how far you want to go from here is dependent entirely on how tired you are. If you want to take a break for lunch, then you can go to

Natraj, Surya Mahal or **Niros**, on the right side of the road, opposite the *lassiwallah*. All serve excellent Indian and continental food.

If you wish to continue after lunch then go on to **Tholia's Kuber** with its collection of silver jewellery and precious and semi precious gems. A few shops away, on the same side, is **Gem Palace** established in 1852 and among the first few to open a showroom on M.I.Road in the early 1900s. It has a rich collection of gems and jewellery as well as an enviable collection of old black and white photographs. Royalty, politicians as well as film stars from all over the world visit this showroom. It is certainly worth a look.

The Mughals brought sophisticated design and new technical know-how with them

Gem Palace

and Jaipur has the best of both worlds. It has been a major centre for production of fine jewellery that is a true blend of Mughal and Rajasthani design and

craftsmanship. The city's jewellers are renowned for jewellery in old silver, gold, lac, precious and semi precious stones. M.I. Road has several shops where you can get traditional as well as contemporary designs.

Further down the road, past the big Bata showroom is the famous **P M Allahbuksh**, an old antiques dealer who has been in the business since 1880 and established this

showroom on M.I.Road in 1913. He has studiously resisted revamping or modernising his shop and it still exudes a late 1950s, early '60s charm.

The walk ends here and you can either go back for lunch or carry on exploring M.I.Road some more. Taxis, scooter/cycle rickshaws are easily available here.

Top: M.I.Road
Left & Below: P M Allahbuksh, a shop dealing in antiques.

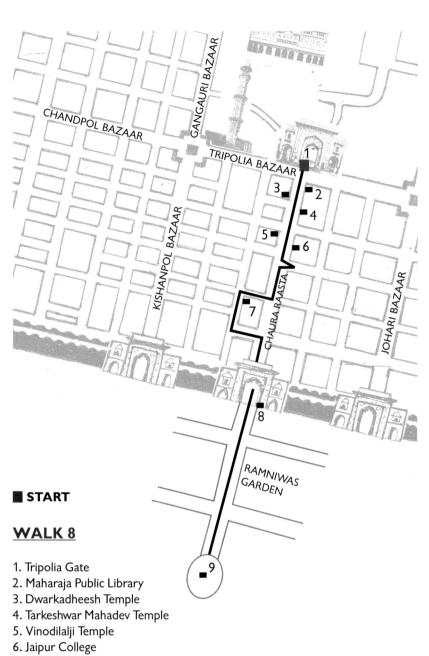

START

WALK 8

1. Tripolia Gate
2. Maharaja Public Library
3. Dwarkadheesh Temple
4. Tarkeshwar Mahadev Temple
5. Vinodilalji Temple
6. Jaipur College
7. Sanjay Sharma Museum
8. New Gate
9. Albert Hall Museum

WALK 8

TRIPOLIA GATE — ALBERT HALL MUSEUM

Busy, new, narrow, crowded lanes but full of life as people go about their daily business. Watch the utensil makers shape brass and iron into traditional pots and pans. Walk past old temples and painted havelies and get a feel of how much thought has gone into the planning of this marvellous city. Visit a private museum in one of the by-lanes.

PARKING

Ample parking is available near Tripolia Gate. It is best to have your car drop you here and meet you at the Albert Hall Museum.

PLACES OF INTEREST

Tripolia Gate – Maharaja Public Library – Tarkeshwar Mahadev Mandir – Potter – Chaura Raasta – Sanjay Sharma Museum – Thatheron ka Raasta – New Gate – Ram Niwas Bagh – Albert Hall Museum

TRIPOLIA GATE

This beautiful triple arched gateway overlooks one of the newer streets in the walled city. You can start your walk from this gate and take a closer look at the enclosed balconies. A security guard posted there is a reminder that this gate is under the care of the Maharaja of Jaipur and for use only by him and his family. The only time this gate interests the local public is during the festivals of Teej and Gangaur because the procession of both come out through this gate on their way to Talkatora where they terminate.

Teej procession

Jaipur has been a city of fairs and festivals. It has been said, quite rightly, that it celebrates nine festivals in seven days. There is a lot of festivity going on in the city throughout the year. The light bulbs, garlands, special welcome gates, *shobhayaatras* are ever existent in the bazaars and streets of the city. There is an added atmosphere of gaiety during the time of festivals.

TEEJ FESTIVAL

Held during the monsoons, July-August, **Teej** is dedicated to **Lord Shiva** and **Parvati.** Women pray for a long and happy married life. Though celebrations are held all over the state, it is particularly colourful in Jaipur. It is the festival when swings are decorated with flowers and hung from trees and young girls and married women dressed in green clothes sing songs to celebrate the advent of monsoon.

Eight men dressed in red clothes carry the palanquin of **Goddess Teejmata** out of Tripolia Gate. Antique gilt palanquins, bullock carts pulling cannons, chariots, gaily decorated elephants with silver howdahs, horses, camels, brass bands, and groups of dancers, all form a part of this grand spectacle. This one kilometre long procession winds its way through the lanes of the old city. Local people come in huge

as people perch on top of buildings and even trees to catch a glimpse of the goddess' idol.

View of Tripolia Gate from Nawab Saheb ki Haveli

numbers, dressed in their best traditional clothes. Groups of men and women can be seen singing, dancing and playing musical instruments, some dressed as gods and goddesses also join in the procession. Space is at a premium

It was for such occasions that the city planners left the terraces over the shops vacant. People still climb up and gather there to get a better view of the processions. This has been a tradition and is followed to this day. There are several areas

around Tripolia gate from where one can get a good view of the colourful procession.

Walk straight ahead with the Tripolia Gate behind you. There are two very interesting buildings on both sides of **Chaura Raasta**, the wide street that lies in front of Tripolia Gate. On the right is one of the oldest hotels in the walled city called **Hind Hotel**. The owners ran into tax problems and had to give up the hotel. It was lying vacant for several years but is now used by the Department of Tourism

as a viewing gallery for tourists during the time of the Gangaur and Teej processions.

On the left is another grand building – the **Maharaja Public Library**. It is a beautifully designed building that could do with some urgent repairs and renovation. It is advisable to just admire it from the outside and move on.

Walk on the left side, but be prepared to cross over to the other side as there are interesting buildings on both sides of the road. The first is a temple on the right – the **Dwarkadheesh Temple** between shop numbers 190-189 followed by another one between 180 – 179. You can cross over for a closer look but there are many more temples on this road and the basic architectural and decorative features remain more or less the same.

Come back to the left side and you can see a temple dedicated to Lord Shiva – the **Tarkeshwar Mahadev Mandir.**

This is one of the most important temples here. A majority of the temples in the walled city are dedicated to Lord Hanuman and the many forms of Lord Krishna.

Tarkeshwar Mahadev temple

This is one of the few temples dedicated to Lord Shiva. It is generally believed on the basis of oral tradition that Shri Tarkeshwarji was an earth born deity. Formally, this was a hamlet occupied by the Meena tribals. Shri Tarkeshwarji is believed to have appeared here and the Meenas then enshrined the deity's image. Just walk in a few steps to get a glimpse of the interiors. It can be a little crowded and so it is best to see it from outside.

You will notice that most of the temples on the main streets are almost always located at a greater height. There are two more temples on the right side, the beautiful Vinodilalji's temple between shop numbers 147-146 and Goverdhan Nathji's temple between shop numbers 137-136. Vinodilalji's temple is worth a closer look. There is a narrow staircase leading up to the temple. Climb up and see the beautiful murals on the exterior walls. Most of them have suffered the ravages of time but some portions are still in fairly good condition. What is unusual about this temple is also the fact that there are not too many buildings with such intricate paintings on the exterior. It is almost always some inner portion of a building where you would find paintings of this nature. Even on this street, there is no other building to match its beauty.

Goverdhannathji's temple

Come back to the left and you will see a big terracotta red building called the Jaipur College. See the building from the outside. What might interest the tourist more is the very exciting collection of terracotta pots spread right on the pavement, outside Jaipur College. It is perhaps one of the most photographed sights on this road. You can pick up a few items if you want because they are quite reasonably priced. Just behind this is **Roop Singh ki Haveli**.

Opposite the Jaipur College is the temple of **Shri Goverdhan Nathji** that was constructed in 1768. The idol worshipped in this temple is that of the childhood form of Lord Krishna. Keep on the left and you will see more buildings in the traditional Jaipur style. Look for the College Book House between shops 241 and 242.

Though this street also has an assortment of shops, it is known more for its bookshops. Close to examination time, temporary stalls come up on the pavements selling guidebooks for schools and colleges. A lot of students can be seen buying and selling books here.

Utensil maker at work

Further down the street, there are coaching classes and tuition centres. As you walk along, you will come across a narrow lane on the left, after shop number 318 called **Sonthli Walon ki Gali**. Walk in a bit. There are some very popular savoury shops here that sell fried salted nuts, chips and gram flour snacks. It is a narrow and crowded lane, so you needn't go beyond this point.

Come out and cross over to the right side of the street. Keep walking on this side until you come to shop number 58 on the right. There is a signboard that says **Sanjay Sharma Museum**. Turn into this lane.

THATHERON KA RAASTA

Thatheron ka Raasta is a lane of the metal utensil makers. A few

Miniature paintings on display at Sanjay Sharma Museum

steps into this lane and you can hear the hammering and beating sounds coming from the various shops. There are around two thousand *thatheras* living here and most of the houses on this lane belong to them. Today, steel has replaced brass and copper utensils and many of the *thatheras* are concentrating on making brass *kalash* for temples. Nevertheless, it is interesting to see these craftsmen using their traditional tools as they shape the utensils.

This is a very short lane and you can walk up to the end of it and come back. Now turn into the first lane on the right. This is still the Thatheron ka Raasta. A modern structure on your left is the **Sanjay Sharma Museum.**

It is a long, narrow, vertical building housing the personal collection of Shri Ram Kripalu Sharma. It is worth a visit as it has a very good collection of miniature paintings, manuscripts and other interesting and rare items.

Come out of the museum and turn left again. You will see more *thatheras* at work in the lane. Keep going straight and turn left when you get to the end of the lane.

You are out in Chaura Raasta again. Keep on the right of the road. The **New Gate** will be visible to you now. As you approach the gate, you will see a cinema hall on the left of the road.

NEW GATE

This is not one of the original seven planned gates of the walled city, it is a later addition. Made during the time of Maharaja Man Singh, it is officially known as the **Man Gate** but popularly called **New Gate**. Though the design of this gate is similar to the others, the sidewalls could not be made due to lack of sufficient space.

Come out through the gate and walk straight ahead to the metal gates. After you have crossed an open ground on the left (unless there is an exhibition on) and a parking lot on the right, you will come to a busy traffic intersection.

Top: Old locks from Sanjay Sharma Museum
Left: The New Gate

Ram Niwas Garden

This is Mirza Ismail Road and the beyond the gates is the **Ram Niwas Bagh** and the clearly visible **Albert Hall Museum.**

RAM NIWAS BAGH

Lush spacious gardens with a zoo, an aviary, a greenhouse, clubs, a herbarium, museum and popular sports ground. Maharaja Ram Singh II laid out these gardens in the year 1868 as a famine relief project for use of the public.

This garden is closest to the walled city and very popular with the inhabitants of the crowded by-lanes who often come here for walks and to eat at the various food stalls. When you approach the fountain, the road on the left leads to the **Ravindra Manch**, an auditorium and the road to the right leads out of the garden. The food stalls are on the right hand corner of this road. **Kiran Café** is famous for *kulfi*.

Straight ahead is the marvellous **Albert Hall Museum.** As you walk towards it, the zoo is on your left and the aviary to your right.

Albert Hall Museum

Detail from Albert Hall Museum

ALBERT HALL MUSEUM

The **Albert Hall Museum** is a brilliant piece of architecture. When the Prince of Wales (later Edward VII) visited Jaipur, Maharaja Ram Singh II was in the midst of laying the Ram Niwas Gardens. He decided to build a permanent memorial of this visit and invited the prince to lay the foundation stone on 6 February 1876. Designed by Sir Swinton Jacob, Albert Hall Museum owes its name to the Victoria and Albert Museum in London and is a happy combination of Rajput, Mughal and European styles of architecture.

This museum provides a splendid introduction to the arts, crafts, and history of Rajasthan. There is a fine collection, which includes handicrafts, such as metal ware, ivory, and woodcarving, jewellery, textiles and pottery, sculptures and paintings. It is particularly rich in brassware. Also on display are life-size models showing scenes from everyday village life.

Exhibits not to be missed are the splendid collection of Jaipur glazed pottery, an Egyptian mummy, and the thirty ft by five ft *phad*, a painted cloth scroll that depicts scenes from the life of a Rajasthani folk hero called Pabuji.

The greatest treasure of this museum is housed in the Darbar Hall.

It is the world's largest Persian garden carpet dating back to 1632. This rare carpet is considered to be the oldest and the best of its kind in the world and is kept under lock and key. However, it can be seen on request.

Your walk ends here. You can get a s c o o t e r / c y c l e rickshaw here.

Persian garden carpet

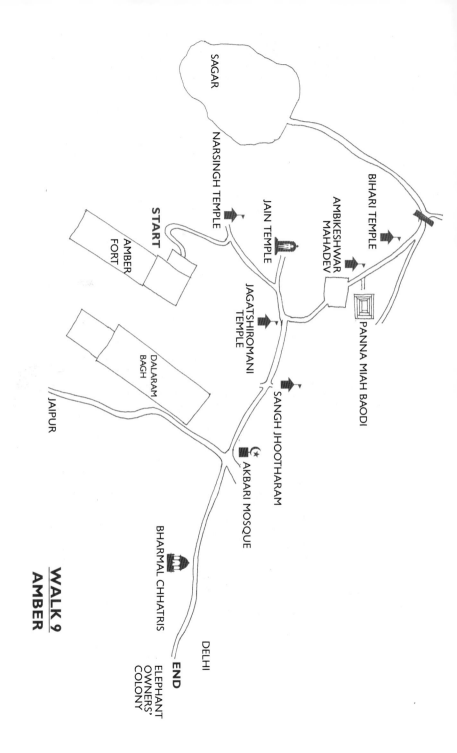

SAGAR

NARSINGH TEMPLE

BIHARI TEMPLE

JAIN TEMPLE

AMBIKESHWAR
MAHADEV

START

AMBER
FORT

JAGATSHIROMANI
TEMPLE

PANNA MIAH BAODI

DALARAM
BAGH

SANGH JHOOTHARAM

JAIPUR

AKBARI MOSQUE

BHARMAL CHHATRIS

DELHI

END

ELEPHANT
OWNERS'
COLONY

WALK 9
AMBER

WALK 9

NARSINGH TEMPLE — BHARMAL KI CHHATRI, AMBER

Lost grandeur, elephants, cobbled streets, ruins of temples and havelies, step wells and the most beautiful lake in Jaipur. Every stone here seems to speak of a bygone era. Very little traffic and a serenity not found in the city. Within the city are numerous fine buildings such as palaces, temples, cenotaphs, mosques, tanks, and wells, dwellings of officials and high priests, and private houses.

A visit to the Amber Fort needs to be done separately as there is much to see there and would require a lot of time. However, you can first visit the fort and walk down from there to explore this township and see its various temples and deserted havelies.

HISTORY

Little is known of the history of Amber before the advent of the Kachchawas. It was under the control of the Susawat Mina tribe. There are hardly any remains worth mentioning that can be ascribed to the Meena chiefs and it seems probable that the home of the Amber Rajas must have been somewhat insignificant before the sixteenth century AD.

Among the well-known rulers of Amber were Raja Baharmal (AD 1547-1573), Raja Man Singh (AD 1589-1614) Mirza Raja Jai Singh (AD 1621-1667) and the founder of Jaipur – Sawai Jai Singh II (AD 1699-1743).

Jai Singh II moved his capital to the new city, and Amber was abandoned almost three hundred years ago because the existing population of nobles and their attendants moved with the court to the new city of Jaipur. By AD 1731, the history of the Kachchawahs shifted from Amber to Jaipur and Amber was reduced to a ghost town.

PARKING

There is a lot of parking space available near the bus stand. It is a very busy road as it leads to the main highway to Delhi. If you are coming from Jaipur, then it is a good idea to park near the entrance of the road that leads to the old township. If you wish to visit the fort first, then you can do that and then walk down from the rear of the fort. There is parking space there.

PLACES OF INTEREST

Narsingh Temple – Digambar Jain Temple – Jagat Shiromani Temple – Ambikeshwar Mahadev Mandir – Panna Mian ka Kund – Sagar – Sanghi Jootha Ram Mandir – Laxmi Narayan Mandir Akbari Mosque – Bharmal ki Chhatri.

THE WALK

There has been rapid, unplanned activity in Amber in

View of Amber town

Amber Fort

recent years. Yet, some vestiges of its past remain. Walk on the few cobbled streets that still remain, going past ruined havelies and old temples, and it will be as if one is walking into the past. There are many other minor ruins of havelies and temples scattered all over the old township. Some are being reused while others have just been left untouched. This town is best explored on foot; the lanes are narrow and comparatively free of traffic. Things may change drastically in a few years, so see it now before all traces of its history are lost forever.

Walk down from the rear entrance of the fort and as you get to the base of the hill, turn left.

Located behind the fort is the abandoned palace of the Kachchawa rulers, commonly known as the **Narsinghji Temple**. It is one of the few protected monuments in this area but do not expect too much from it. It's importance is more historical than architectural, as this was the first palace of the Kachchawas. This

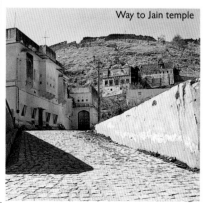
Way to Jain temple

was their home before they moved to the larger, more elegant Amber Palace.

Built by Raja Narsingh Dev (1388-1428) in the early fifteenth century, the temple occupies a small portion of the structure. Within the rooms that were once used for ceremonial purposes are the **Rajtilak ki Chhatri**, where the rulers were anointed, and the *Balabai ki Saal* where important rituals connected to marriages took place.

Get the caretaker who is on duty here, to show you around.

Come out of the temple and go straight on the road heading eastwards. When you get to the T-junction, turn left first and go up the slope to the **Sanwalaji Ka Mandir** better known as the **Digambar Jain Mandir.**

This seventeenth century temple can be seen mainly for its design and location because thoroughly modern restoration has taken away quite a bit of its beauty.

Walk down from this temple and you will see a ruined temple on the left. Go past this and when you get to the lane from where you turned left, see the building on the right corner. This is one of the most

One of the several temples in Amber

beautiful temples in Amber – the **Jagat Shiromani** temple.

Take off your shoes and walk up the stairs for a closer look because this temple, more than any other, deserves a closer look.

The **Jagat Shiromani** temple is famous for its architectural beauty. It was constructed in the sixteenth century by Man Singh I in memory of his eldest son, Jagat Singh. The temple has images of Lord Vishnu as well as Radha and Krishna. Legend has it that in the sixteenth century, the saint-poetess Mira Bai, a devotee of Lord Krishna, brought this idol with her from Chittaurgarh. The temple has

Jagat Shiromani temple

a remarkable *toran*, or gateway, with elaborate carvings on its marble pillars and columns.

Chomu Haveli

Walk back to the street and take the straight narrow lane going northwards. A few remnants of the old buildings can be seen here. Keep to the road until it gets you to a large open area known as **Ambikeshwar Chowk**.

This is a community space for the town, with a well, huge trees and two temples close to each other. The one on the left is **Rameshwarji ka Mandir,** a seventeenth century temple dedicated to Lord Ram. Next to it is the sixteenth century **Ambikeshwar Mahadev** temple, one of Amber's oldest temples.

AMBIKESHWAR MAHADEV

The origins of this temple, dedicated to Lord Shiva, are obscure. It has carved marble pillars and marble flooring. The temple lies ten feet below ground level and if local legend is to be believed, then the temple is sinking and may not be around for too long. Legend also has it that Amber got its name from this temple. If you want to have a closer look, take off your shoes at the entrance and go in. It is not crowded like other temples but attracts a large number of devotees during **Shivratri**, Lord Shiva's birth celebrations.

To the north, and overlooking the quiet and peaceful courtyard where the Ambikeshwar temple is located, lies the **Panna Miah Ka Kund**. Come out of the temple and walk towards the narrow lane on the left. Just after the turning, the lane widens and the entrance to the kund is on the right. Go in through this arched gateway and climb the few steps on the left.

Ambikeshwar Mahadev Temple

PANNA MIAH KA KUND

Built in the seventeenth century by Panna Miah, a eunuch and leading official at the court of Raja Jai Singh II, it is square shaped with octagonal kiosks at the four corners and a double storied veranda.

These step-wells are unique to this side of the country where water was always in short supply. This is one of the better-preserved wells in this area and this huge man-made water reservoir was used for both drinking and bathing purposes and has a flight of steps leading down to the water level. This tank has been partly restored and is still used by the local people and their animals. Soon after rains, this becomes a swimming pool for the local boys who dare each other to jump from the highest point possible.

From the *kund* if you walk eastwards, the cobbled path will take you past some more ruined temples and havelies and then out through the **Kheri Gate**, one of the old gates of Amber. The **Sagar** is a popular picnic spot and located just behind Jaigarh fort, in a depression formed by the surrounding hills. It consists of two terraced lakes that

Panna Miah ka Kund

stand. Further on the road, on the left is another protected monument–the **Sanghi Juntharam** Temple.

SANGHI JUNTHARAM TEMPLE

This is one of Amber's more important temples. It was originally a Jain temple but was later converted into a Saivite one. Mohandas, the prime minister of Mirza Raja Singh I, built it in AD 1657. Juntharam, a descendant of Mohandas, made additions in later years and hence the name. It stands on a high platform and has some very fine carving on its inner walls. At one time, it had a beautiful twelve-sided well, a small garden and several chambers. Today, most of it is ruined but one can catch a glimpse of its past glory.

were once important sources of water supply at times of siege. The stepped fortification walls descend to the lake and there are traces of an elaborate water transport system here, through which the water was taken up by elephants. There is a small nondescript temple here but the lush green hilly slopes between **Kheri Gate** and **Sagar** are a walker's delight.

Come back the same way, and go towards the **Jagat Shiromani** temple and turn left when you get to the T-junction. This is the road that will lead you towards the bus

Sanghi Juntharam Temple

mementoes, teashops and restaurants selling bottled soft drinks and local sweets, is the beautiful **Laxmi Narayan** temple. There is also a *kos minar* located here. There is encroachment all around but worth a look.

Carry on the same road and you will be out of the town on the Jaipur-Delhi road.

The main market and the Amber bus stand are located on this road. Hidden behind shops selling

When you come out on this busy road, keep to the left and you will find another lane turning in to the left. A few steps in and you will find an imposing **Jain** temple on the left. It is in fairly good condition and has many carved panels and pillars.

Come back and continue your walk towards another major monument—**The Akbari Mosque.**

Akbari Mosque

It was built it in AD 1569. Akbar is believed to have stopped here to pray while he was on his way to the Dargah in Ajmer. The mosque has been repaired several times in the past but the basic structure remains unchanged.

Come out on to the main road and further down this road, again towards the west, is a walled enclosure that was the old burial ground for the rulers of Amber – **Bharmal ki Chhatri**.

CHHATRIS

There is a group of 'chhatris' or cenotaphs in different shapes and sizes. Some are twelve sided, some circular and others square with porticos on their four sides. All of them have domes crowned by finials. Their ceilings are very interesting – concentric rings of overlapping stones, with beautiful pendants hanging from their centres.

After the seat of power was moved to Jaipur, this was abandoned and a new spot established at Gaitor. Though one

One of the several chhatris in the complex

can still see a carved pillar here and a hint of wall painting there, most of the cenotaphs lie in ruins. They are neither dated nor is it known which *chhatri* belongs to which ruler.

Walk a little more on this road, and then cross over to the other side of the road. This area would be of special interest to animal lovers. This is a colony of elephant owners. Watch them being fed and bathed and painted if it is a special occasion. Elephants from here take the tourists up to Amber, go as part of marriage processions, and participate in the elephant festival.

It may interest you to know that there are around eighty-eight elephants in Jaipur, and this is just one of the colonies where they live. While you are here, ask for the elephant that greeted former US president, Bill Clinton!

The walk ends here and you can head back to the bus stand where it is possible to get scooter rickshaws.

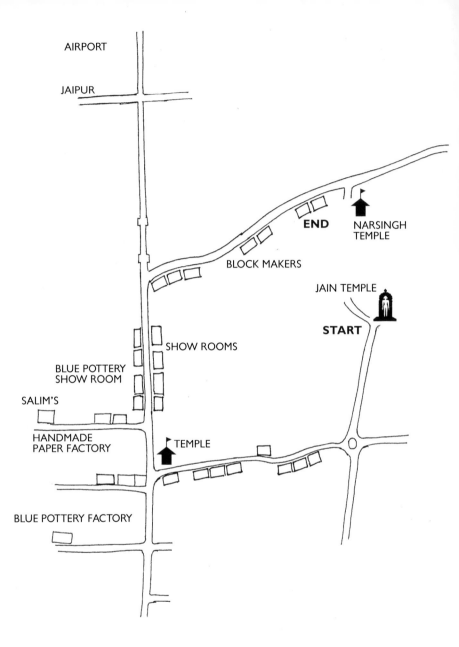

AIRPORT

JAIPUR

END

NARSINGH
TEMPLE

BLOCK MAKERS

JAIN TEMPLE

START

SHOW ROOMS

BLUE POTTERY
SHOW ROOM

SALIM'S

HANDMADE
PAPER FACTORY

TEMPLE

BLUE POTTERY FACTORY

WALK 10
SANGANER

WALK 10

DIGAMBAR JAIN TEMPLE — NARSINGH TEMPLE, SANGANER

Sanganer was named after a Kachchawa prince, Sangaji and is sixteen km to the south of Jaipur and well known for its handicrafts. It is an important centre for craft, industry and produces some of the finest handmade paper, hand block printed textiles and screen printers. Both handmade paper and textiles are popular all over the country and abroad. The town has several ruins and interesting old havelies dating back to the sixteenth century. An old eleventh century Jain temple with fine carvings is also worth visiting.

PLACES OF INTEREST

Jain temples – Blue Pottery – Handmade Paper – Block Printers – Block Makers.

PARKING

It is a good idea to start this walk from the Digambar Jain temple and to take your taxi, scooter rickshaw all the way to the temple and walk out of the town from there.

Drive across the bridge that leads to Sanganer town and turn to the left immediately after a fairly large but ruined old building on the main road. You cannot miss it because this is the only traditional looking building amidst all the modern structures on this road. When you get to a traffic roundabout, turn left again and you will find yourself near the **Digambar Jain** temple. Your car can meet you near **Shilpi Handicrafts** located on the road that turns left immediately after the bridge.

This is not a planned town so do not expect any straight roads, neat colonies and uniform shops. This is mainly a village of craftsmen that has grown in a rather unplanned way to accommodate the mushrooming showrooms that line the main streets.

SHRI DIGAMBAR JAIN MANDIR

The most beautiful temple in Sanganer is the ancient **Shri Digambar Jain** temple. It has very fine carvings that bring to mind those of the magnificent Dilwara temples of Mount Abu. Built in various phases with high *shikharas* (spires), the temple represents the traditional style of architecture. The last phase was probably built in the tenth century. The beautiful *nij-mandir* (inner temple) is a stone shrine with three pinnacles. In the centre is an idol of **Parshwanath** with seven serpent hoods. All around are carvings of lotuses, creepers and elephants pouring water from pitchers held in their trunks. But the main idol is that of **Adinath**, installed in the shrine behind this. You can walk around the temple and explore the huge campus. There is a lot of repair work that has been undertaken by the temple trust and the temple is well maintained and clean.

Digambar Jain temple

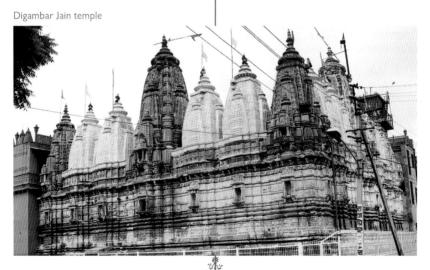

Come out of the temple and go straight towards the traffic roundabout, the way you drove in. Take the right turn from the circle and walk on this lane.

THE LANE

As you walk back towards the outer road, you will see many modern structures on the way. But that is not to say that there is nothing interesting to be found here. There are still a few remnants of the town as it must have been some centuries ago. As you walk past the small shops and houses that open on to the street, you can always count on seeing something that will catch your eye and make you stop and look. Look out for a small white house on the left that stands out for its traditional design and use of original building materials.

Again on the left, a few yards away, is another small house where

Dyer at work

you just might find a couple working seriously to untie several metres of tie and dye fabric. They work oblivious of passers-by and try to stretch the striking pink fabric as quickly as they can. Printers and dyers work mainly on per metre rates and so they try to do as much work in a day as possible.

A typical Sanganeri block print

either side of the arched doorway. The haveli on the left has an intricately painted entrance.

Tie & dye

Soon after this house, there is a ruined old haveli on the left and further ahead are two old havelies on either side of the street. They stand directly opposite each other and are quite large in comparison to the other houses that you will see in this town. The haveli on the right has an interesting gateway with two covered platforms on

BLUE POTTERY

Keep on this lane and very soon you will come to a very old dilapidated building on the right. The road ends here and meets up with the main street that runs from east to west. Turn left on this road and cross over. Right in front is a small blue pottery showroom, one of the oldest in Sanganer. This family has a blue pottery

factory in an adjoining lane so ask somebody at the show room to take you to the factory where you can watch the various stages of blue pottery.

Blue pottery is based on ground quartz. The dough is pressed into moulds and the unfired pieces are hand painted with oxide colours, dipped in clear glaze and fired once in wood kilns. The process is tedious and time consuming. Once made, the blue pottery items cannot be reworked and one never knows if the finished product will have the exact shade one wants.

Today, blue pottery has changed from the traditional flower vases, bowls and huge pots and one can get smaller items like key chains, ash trays and candle stands.

After seeing the factory, come back to the blue pottery showroom and head eastwards and

Potter at work

Paper products

take the first turn into the right lane to see another fascinating local craft – **handmade paper.**

HANDMADE PAPER

The famous *kagazi mohala* (colony of handmade paper makers) is the world's largest centre. In 1728, Maharaja Jai Singh II set up this paper industry in Sanganer where abundant clear water, essential for paper-making was available.

The *kagzis* (papermakers) always enjoyed royal patronage and continued to thrive. Today, there are about ten handmade paper industries in Sanganer and of these the largest is Salim Kagzi's Handmade Paper and Board Industries located towards the end of this road.

It is a huge complex and you cannot miss it even if you try. Walk in and the friendly people here will be happy to show you around and explain the process to you. It may be of interest to know that this product is eco-friendly and is still made the traditional way.

THE PROCESS

This industry plays a major role in re-cycling. It uses all manner of leftovers from cloth to scrap paper, leaves to flower petals, straw to silk threads and produces the most amazing results. The range is very impressive. Over the years, new designs have been introduced and there has been a wider usage. Today, handmade paper is being used in a variety of items from decorative to the functional.

Except for the electric motors used for pulping, calendaring and peripheral activities, all production is manual. No chemicals whatsoever are used. All colouring is organic. Decorative effects are produced by inclusions such as petals, grass clippings and the like. Paper is dried under the sun. The water let out from the industries is benign.

The first step is reducing cotton waste to pulp. Flower petals are added to the pulp, which is then transferred to large tanks. Two workers submerge a rectangular tray of fine mesh into the water just below the surface. Taking pulp from the bottom of the tank, they empty it into the tray and mix it as the pulp settles. The tray is then lifted out of the water and covered with a piece of muslin that is stretched over the sheet of pulp. After inverting the tray and the muslin, the sheet of pulp now on top is added to a pile. The pile is then pressed to drive out most of the water. The resulting sheets are peeled off the muslin and hung out to dry.

Books with blank pages, portfolios, boxes of many different shapes and sizes, pencil boxes,

Paper sheets set out to dry

sheets of paper and more are available to buy in the showroom. These items are lightweight and make great gifts.

Walk back from the paper factory and come on the main street again and turn left. This entire street is lined with showrooms selling the other craft for which Sanganer is famous – hand-block printing. Go in and have a look, the products are quite reasonably priced.

Just before you approach the bridge, there is a lane that turns right. Go down this lane and you can see the block makers and printers at work. As you explore the market, look out for tractor trolleys carrying bales of colourfully printed fabric from one location to another. You can ask to see the entire process, from block making to printing, dyeing and drying – it all happens here.

HANDBLOCK PRINTING

The handblock printing industry in Sanganer has flourished for centuries even though its origin as a textile-producing centre remains shrouded in mystery. However, it

Block printing

Skilled block printer at work

is quite apparent that this industry received royal patronage when it was set up. It has grown enormously today and the signs are there to see in the open areas in and around Sanganer that are full of printed fabric left to dry on the ground or dyed and suspended from huge wooden frames.

You can see them all around you as you walk on this street that goes along the dry riverbed. Also on this lane are block makers, printers, dyers and driers.

Block Making – Expert block makers use local wood to carve the most exquisite designs that are then handed over to the printer. And it is not just one block per design, sometimes there are as many as thirty separate blocks needed for one design.

Printing — Printing is an elaborate process; each yard of printed fabric may need up to 350 separate impressions. Patterns

Wooden blocks that are used for printing

The finished product ready for sale

mainly depict flowers, gods, elephants, camels, birds and dolls as well as geometric designs. The printing is done on sturdy wooden tables and it is very interesting to see the expertise with which this whole process is undertaken.

DYEING

Reams of dyed cloth are hung on racks to dry. Black dyes are prepared by fermenting iron oxide with molasses and gum; red by extracting alizarin from madder roots and mixing with a local flower in lukewarm water in a large copper pot; blue from indigo extracted from the leaves of the *neel* plant (*indigofera tinctoria*); yellow from pomegranate rind and raw turmeric. Unfortunately, chemical dyes have replaced the natural colours, screens have joined blocks and buyers themselves who know and understand their market best are supplying designs regularly.

The mill made bleached cloth is prepared for handblock printing by washing and shrinking for several hours.

Shri Narsingh Temple that you may see briefly as it is among the older monuments in Sanganer. There is not much that has been preserved but gives a rather good idea about the kind of buildings that existed in the earlier years.

Your walk ends here.

Drying — The printed pieces of cloth are dried in the sun and after the dyes are fixed, the cloth is given one or more washes and finally sized and dried before it is ready for the market.

The printer produces a wide range of fabrics in bright colours and attractive designs that are made into saris, *odhnis*, bedcovers and tablecloths.

After you have had your fill of Sanganeri printing, go further, past a huge sign on the left that says **Shilpi** until you get to a rather dilapidated building on the first right lane after Shilpi. It is a corner building but the entrance is a few yards into the lane. This is the

ADDITIONAL INFORMATION ON JAIPUR

Palace on Wheels

GETTING TO JAIPUR

By Air
Sanganer Airport, 11 km from the city center is the main air gateway to Jaipur. There are direct flights to Delhi, Mumbai, Udaipur, Jodhpur, Aurangabad, and some other cities from Jaipur.

By Rail
From Delhi, there are many trains that connect Jaipur and other cities in Rajasthan; foremost among them is the Palace on Wheels. Other important trains include Shatabdi Express and Pink City Express both from Delhi. There are good trains to and from Bombay, Ahmedabad, Agra and Kolkata as well.

By Road
From Delhi, there is a direct and well-maintained road to Jaipur. It is connected to most of the tourist destinations in Rajasthan as well as Agra. Jaipur is part of the Golden Triangle of India that includes Delhi, Agra, and Jaipur.

SOME PLACES TO STAY IN JAIPUR

FIVE STAR HOTELS

FIVE STAR HOTELS	EMAIL ADDRESS	TELEPHONE #	ADDRESS
Raj Mahal Palace	——	(0141) 2381625; 2381757	Sardar Patel Marg
Clarks Amer Hotel	clarksamer@eth.net	2550616; fax:2550013	JLN Marg
Jai Mahal Palace	jaimahal.jaipur@tajhotels.com	2223636	Jacob Road
Rambagh Palace	rambagh.jaipur@tajhotels.com	2381919	Sawai Ram Singh Road
Hotel Mansingh Palace & Towers	mansingh.jaipur@mailcity.com	2378771	Sansarchandra Road
Hotel Trident (Oberoi's)	reservations@tridentjp.com	2670101	Amer Road

HERITAGE HOTELS

HERITAGE HOTELS	EMAIL ADDRESS	TELEPHONE #	ADDRESS
Mandawa Haveli	reservations@castlemandawa.com	2371194	Sansar Chandra Road
Samode Haveli	reservations@samode.com	2632370; 2632407	Ganga Pole
Narain Niwas	tushjit@sancharnet.in	2570811; 2562735	Narain Singh Circle
Alsisar Haveli	alsisar@satyam.net.in	2364652; 2364685	Sansar Chandra Road
Bissau Palace	bissau@sancharnet.in	2304371	Outside Vhandpole Gate
Arya Niwas	tarun@aryaniwas.com	2372456	Sansar Chandra Road
General's Retreat	bist@generalsretreat.com	2377134	Sardar Patel Marg
Loharu House	——	2225251	Civil Lines
Hotel Saket	hotelsaket@yahoo.com	2381791; 2383533	Tilak Marg, C-Scheme
Hotel Maharani Palace	maharani@sancharnet.in	2204702-7; 2204378	Station Road
Hotel Meru Palace	merupalace@hotmail.com	2371111-16	Ram Singh Road
Hotel Jasvilas	info@jasvilas.com	2204638	Banipark

FAIRS & FESTIVALS CALENDAR 2004-2010

Fairs & Festivals	Place	Tithi	2004	2005	2006	2007	2008	2009	2010
Camel Festival	Bikaner	Paush-Shukla (14-15)	6-7 Jan.	24-25 Jan.	13-14 Jan.	2-3 Jan.	21-22 Jan.	10-11 Jan.	31 Dec., 1st Jan.
Brij Festival	Bharatpur	-	2-4 Feb.	2-4 Feb.	2-4 Feb.	2-4 Feb.	2-4 Feb.	2-4 Feb.	2-4 Feb.
Alwar Festival	Alwar	-	13-15 Feb.	11-13 Feb.	10-12 Feb.	9-11 Feb.	8-10 Feb.	13-15 Feb.	12-14 Feb.
Nagaur Cattle Fair	Nagaur	Magh-s (7-10)	28-31 Jan.	15-18 Feb.	4-7 Feb.	25-28 Feb.	13-16 Feb.	2-5 Feb	22-25 Feb
Desert Festival	Jaisalmer	Magh-s(13-15)	4-6 Feb.	21-23 Feb.	10-12 Feb.	31 Jan.-2Feb.	19-21 Feb.	7-9 Feb	28-30 Jan.
Baneshwar Fair	Baneshwar (Dungarpur)	Magh-s (11-15)	1-5 Feb.	19-23 Feb.	8-12 Feb.	29 Jan.-2 Feb.	17-21 Feb.	5-9 Feb.	26-30 Jan.
Elephant Festival	Jaipur	Phalgun-s-15	6 March	25 March	14 March	3 March	21 March	10 March	28 March
Shitala Ashtami	Chaksu, Jaipur	Chaitra k-8	13 March	1 April	23 March	12 March	28 March	19 March	8 March
Kailadevi Fair	Karauli	Chaitra-s (3-4)	23-24 March	11-12 April	1-2 April	21-22 March	8-9 April	29-30 March	18-19 March
Gangaur Festival	Jaipur	Chaitra-s (3-5)	23-25 March.	11-13 April	1-3 April	21-23 March	8-10 April	29-31 March	18-20 March
Mewar Festival	Udaipur	Chaitra k-12	18 March	6 April	26 March	16 March	3 April	23 March	12 March
Mahavirji Fair	Mahavirji	Chaitra-s (9-15)	30 March-5 April	18-24 April	7-13 April	27 March-2 April	14-20 April	3-9 April	24-30 April
Summer Festival	Mt. Abu	Baisakh (13-Buddh Purnima)	2-4 May	21-23 May	11-13 May	30 April-2 May	18-20 May	7-9 May	26-28 May
Teej Festival	Jaipur	Shravan-s (3-4)	19-20 Aug.	8-9 Aug.	28-29 July	15-16 Aug.	4-5 Aug.	24-25 July	12-13 Aug.
Kajli Teej	Bundi	Bhadra-k (2-3)	31 Aug.-1 Sept.	20-21 Aug.	11-12 Aug.	30-31 Aug.	18-19 Aug.	8-9 Aug.	26-27 Aug.
Ramdevra Fair	Pokaran (Jaisalmer)	Bhadra-s (9-10)	22-23 Sept.	12-13 Sept.	2-3 Sept.	21-22 Sept.	9-10 Sept.	29-30 Aug.	17-18 Sept.
Marwar Festival	Jodhpur	Aswin-s (14-15)	26-27 Oct.	16-17 Oct	6-7 Oct.	25-26 Oct.	13-14 Oct.	3-4 Oct.	21-22 Oct.
Dussehra Festival	Kota	Aswin-s(8-10)	20-22 Oct.	10-12 Oct.	30 Sept.-2 Oct.	19-21 Oct.	7-9 Oct.	26-28 Sept.	15-17 Oct.
Pushkar Fair	Pushkar (Ajmer)	Kartik-s(8-15)	18-26 Nov.	8-15 Nov.	29 Oct.-5 Nov.	17-24 Nov.	5-13 Nov.	25 Oct. 02 Nov.	13-21 Nov.
Chandrabhaga Fair	Jhalawar	Kartik-s 14 Magh-k 1	25-27 Nov.	14-16 Nov.	4-6 Nov.	23-25 Nov.	12-14 Nov.	1-3 Nov.	20-22 Nov.
Kolayat Fair	Kolayat (Bikaner)	Kartik-s11 Magh-k 5	22 Nov.-1 Dec.	12-21 Nov.	1-9 Nov.	20-29 Nov.	9-18 Nov.	29 Oct-7 Nov.	17-26; Nov.
Winter Festival	Mt.Abu	-	29-31 Dec.	29-31 Dec.	29-31 Dec.	29-31 Dec.	29-31 Dec.	29-31 Dec.	29-31 Dec.

PHOTO CREDITS

Maps and line drawings: **K P Singh**.

Photographs: **Sudhir Kasliwal**: Pages 78, 79, 100 (top) and 102 (bottom).

M D Sharma: Pages 25 (bottom), 26 (top), 27 (bottom), 35 (top), 100 (bottom), 106 (top) and 121 (top).

Narendra Sain: Pages 48 (top), 109, 111, 112 (top) and 114.

A S Jhala: Pages 62, 74, 81, 86, 87, 101 and 103.

Dharmendar Kanwar: Pages 118 to 127.

Old black & white city pictures courtesy **Evelyn Bazalgette**.

Arisia Diamond Collection: Page 47 (top).

Pictures courtesy: *Indian Carpets* and *A Jewelled Splendour,* Rupa & Co.: Page 115.

INDEX